Freedom

From Mind to Awareness

Gopalakrishnan Kulasekaran

ISBN 978-93-5667-194-2
© Gopalakrishnan Kulasekaran 2022
Published in India 2022 by Pencil

A brand of
One Point Six Technologies Pvt. Ltd.
123, Building J2, Shram Seva Premises,
Wadala Truck Terminal, Wadala (E)
Mumbai 400037, Maharashtra, INDIA
E connect@thepencilapp.com
W www.thepencilapp.com

Author biography

Gopalakrishnan K (GK) is one of India's premier speakers on Yoga and Personal Mastery. GK is passionate about human potential and raising the consciousness of human potential to its height. As a presenter, GK has the rare ability to electrify the audience and yet deliver uncommonly original and useful insights that lead individuals to raise their awareness and move from the mind which moves from one sensation to another to awareness which is inward, deeper, and deeper.

Worked as an IT Consultant for nearly 20 years for many of the most well-known organizations across the globe.

CONTENTS

Preface

What one observes in our life and others is that one of the main reasons people feel stressed or Anger is because they feel life is not going the way they desired. This causes many to feel de-motivated, anxious, stressed, and sometimes depressed.

Mind is the only tool through which we experience our emotions and through which we interact with the external world. But the mind waxes and wanes like the moon and is not stable. Hence there is always a sense of uncertainty. The main reason for this is we are disconnected from who we are actually. Our mind has been conditioned by the society and hence we don't actually realize what will give us real joy and happiness.

A mind conditioned by society will always think wealth and power will give us joy and happiness.

Hence there is a need to understand about the society in which we live and the first chapter is about society. The next chapter titled "World, Maya and God" is about the reality of life which is nothing but the continuous strife in our lives and this leads to a lack of aliveness among people and they take refuge in religion. But Religion or priest is not able to liberate them they just get hypnotized and isolated then become free.

Before we make the journey towards creating a stable platform we need to know about ourselves and the third chapter is about "Self-knowledge". Any platform that we create within us must be built with things we already possess and the only thing which we have is our body, mind, emotion, and energy. The next four chapters [Mind, Body, Energy and Emotion] is about those four things.

All our actions in this world are outbound and when we work with machines and technology we slowly disconnect with our life and our consciousness and we become mechanical, just like machines. So to connect to our real self we need to dive into meditation and meditation does not mean just sitting in a room closing our eyes, it also means awareness about ourselves in action which is nothing but awareness of our relationship with people. Meditation is like a wave that starts from outside and moves inside us and transformation can only happen within us as the external environment is beyond our control. Transformation can happen only if we are aware of it, most of us are unconscious of our inner world. Mediation and awareness are the next two chapters.

Once we become aware of our mind and the depth of our consciousness will increase, the Mind instead of moving from one sensation to another will turn inwards and our consciousness will become deeper. Awareness with great depth will lead to Freedom which is the final chapter.

The book is the outcome of my own experience and knowledge got from many amazing people and it is my wish and blessing that it should bring transformation in the lives of all the people who read it.

Chapter 1 Individual and Society

Society

The action of the relationship between me and others is – Society. When we say it is a capitalist, communist or fascist society, surely it has not come up by itself. All the misery and confusion that we see around us has not come up by itself. We have created it in our relationship with each other. What we are has been projected outside.

If we are miserable, confused, and chaotic within, the projection of that outside of us has become the world or society. Society is the product of our relationships and if our relationship is narrow, confused, egocentric, and limited, then its projection outside — our world is surely going to be chaotic. Surely, this is a simple fact. But we want to bring about an alteration in this, through a system or through an idea outside of us, forgetting that it is we who have created this society. So, the transformation has to begin with us. We have to become the change that we want to see in this world.

What is the relationship of the individual to society? Nobody has paid much attention to the individual and it seems to be the root cause of all problems. This is because the individual seems to be so small while the society seems so big. People think that if we can change society, then the individuals will also change. But this has never happened in history because 'society' is only a word. Without individuals, there can be no society. Society has no soul and is static. We cannot change anything in it. We can only change the individual howsoever small he appears. Once you know the science of how to change the individual, it can be applied to all individuals. Society exists for the individual and not the other way round.

Society exists for the fruition of man. It exists to give freedom to an individual so that he may have the opportunity to awaken the highest intelligence. This intelligence is not the mere cultivation of a technique or knowledge or something to be achieved by following a book or a Process. It is to be in touch with that creative reality that is not of the superficial mind. Intelligence is not a cumulative result, but the freedom from progressive achievement and success. Intelligence is never static; it cannot be copied and standardized and hence cannot be taught. Intelligence is to be discovered in freedom.

Society is a reflection of the human mind

This incident is said to have happened in the life of Emperor Akbar.

He had built a very beautiful marble pond. He had brought swans specially from 'Man Sarovar', in the Himalayas. He wanted to have the pond filled with milk, not water, as it was an emperor's pond. Everybody in the capital was to be informed that one bucket of milk from every house was to reach the palace early next morning just before sunrise. Birbal, his minister, told Akbar, "You don't understand the human mind at all. Your pond will be full of water."

Akbar was surprised to hear this and asked how that was possible because it was an order from the emperor that nobody could dare to refuse. Birbal replied, "Let us wait until tomorrow and see". The next morning, emperor Akbar and his minister Birbal, went to the garden and found the pond full of water. Akbar was shocked and asked, "This is strange. How did it happen? Catch a few people from the street, whoever is available and ask how this happened." A few people were caught and questioned and they said, "The truth is, we thought the whole capital would bring buckets of milk. One bucket of water would be completely overlooked. Nobody would ever know. But now, we see that the pond is full of water." It seems that everybody had the same thought in the whole capital! Not a single man is different.

The human mind functions exactly the same. So, before we criticize society, we must understand that it is our human mind creating it and we are contributing our bucketful of misery. No revolution can be successful unless the human mind is understood by us and transformation happens at the mind level. Everybody is hoping that "My bucketful of water is not going to be noticed at all". If everybody understands that this idea is what will come to every human mind and decides, "At least, I should bring a bucketful of milk. I should not behave in an unconscious way like all human beings are behaving, then it would be possible to have a pond full of milk". The world or the society is an extension of ourselves. If we, as an individual, desire to destroy hate, then as an individual, we must cease hating. To destroy hate, we must disassociate ourselves from hate in all its gross and subtle forms. So long as we are caught up in it and are a part of that world of ignorance and fear, nothing will change.

The world is nothing but an extension of ourselves, duplicated and multiplied. Society does not exist apart from the individual. It may exist as an idea, as a state, as a social organization, but to carry out that idea, to make that social or religious organization function, there must be an individual. Individuals' ignorance and greed and fear, maintain the structure of ignorance, greed, and hate. If we as an individual change, this change impacts the entire world.

Authority and Individual

A person who wants to transform himself always relies on religious books or authority to understand himself. There is no clear path for inner journey and hence people rely on books and spiritual gurus to guide them. But the most important thing is — Can self-knowledge be given by others or learned through books?

The reason for the failure of many self-help books to actually help people is not that the authors of the books were not an authority in their field or that they were not sincere enough. It is just that books can only give information or knowledge. But for real transformation to happen, it has to be applied by the individual themselves in their life.

The state or an organization does not need individuality, it needs efficiency. So, the more individual a person becomes, the less useful he is considered to society and the more dangerous, as he begins to think outside the conditioning of society. The whole pattern of our civilization and in fact, of all civilizations that have existed in the world, is to turn the human being into an automaton or robot. A mechanical mind will follow the pattern prescribed by the Church or a political establishment. The Person will be obedient, efficient, and not dangerous. Otherwise, a mind that is inventive, inquiring, seeking, searching for the new and always trying to give birth to something unknown, is bound to create disturbances. He will become a rebel and the political establishment cannot be at ease with him.

To be a free man and to exist in any society is very difficult, as society does not want any free man. A free man is a danger to society's existence as he is not conforming to the ideology or rules set by it. Hence, the free man is seen as a rebel or threat to society.

Conditioning of the society

A child does not have any self-image or opinion about itself. But as a child grows in society, he is conditioned by the society about what is good and bad based on the culture of that society, at that particular time. The child then tries to shape himself to an image considered as good by that society.

As long as the child fits into the image, he is treated well by society. Else, he is considered a pariah, and society ostracises him from that community. Hence, a child is never allowed to develop his own individuality by society.

Before a child becomes seven years of age, his individuality is killed completely. Only if by chance, the establishment is not successful in doing this, can a person become an individual. But this is rare. Every type of social institution is a means of killing the individual and converting him into a machine.

A society feels safe only if a man can be predicted if it knows what he can do and what he will do. We can predict a husband, a wife, a doctor, a lawyer or a scientist. We know who they are and how they will react. We can be at ease with them. But it is impossible to be at ease with a person who is alive and spontaneous because we don't know what he will do. He is unpredictable.

Unpredictability is always a source of insecurity. A wife cannot be at ease with a husband who is unpredictable. The moment he is unpredictable, he is unmanageable. He cannot be manipulated. No one is at ease with an unpredictable person — not even a father with an unpredictable son.

But only the unpredictable man can feel happiness, can feel ease like no one else. Life itself is unpredictable and unmanageable. Life as such always moves from moment to moment towards the unknown. It is an opening into the unknown — nothing more, nothing less.

Creativity

We don't need historians to say that our society is crumbling and that one of the fundamental reasons for this is that individuals have ceased to be creative.

Our daily existence of earning our livelihood, getting jobs, earning money, our relationship in the family, constantly trying to become more, our desires, ambitions have all drained our mind. It is surely a tired and bitter mind, filled with envy, full of desires that cannot have love in it.

A tired mind is not a creative mind. We have become imitative. We are copying. Copying an outward technique is fine and necessary to a certain extent but when there is an inward psychological imitation, we cease to be creative. Our education, social structure, religious life is all based on imitation. We have become a mere repetitive, mechanical machine with certain conditioned responses, according to the pattern of society, and this is one of the fundamental reasons that we have ceased to become creative. We can see that there is disintegration when there is imitation. When there is authority, there must be imitation, whether it is the authority of the Church or the authority of a book. All of us at some point in life have had moments of creativeness, happy moments of vital interest, where there is no sense of repetition, no sense of copying. Such moments are always new, fresh, creative, and happy. So, one of the fundamental causes of the disintegration of society is copying which translated into action is worshiping of authority.

Chapter 2 Humans, Maya, and God

Understanding Maya is important. Without a correct understanding of the world we live in, we will conclude things about it based on our experience and the karmic memory that we have inherited.

What we call our life is nothing but the experience created by our mind based on our relationship with others and our position in society. It takes a person with certain awareness and intelligence to understand that both the relationship with others and our position in this society are not fixed and changes with time. This makes our experience of life also change and therefore, sometimes we are optimistic, while at other times, we are a pessimistic.

When an individual is young, he is an optimist and the world appears to be a wonderful place to live. But as he grows older and faces hardship in making a living and maintaining a relationship, he slowly becomes a pessimist.

If one truly sees that the world has no real existence of its own and exists only in relationship with our mind, then his entire perspective will change. He will no longer be influenced by of other people's opinions and become interested in his own reaction to it as that only determines his experience. This is the reason different people have different ideas or opinions of the world even though we live in the same physical world. We ourselves have different opinions of the world at different stages of our own life.

Crystallization

What we need is a stable platform — as the basic need of the mind is security and stability. The external world can never give this stability as it is bound to wax and wane, whether it is our position in the world or our relationship with others. Hence, a stable mind can only be created within us, internally. What all of us have is our body, mind, emotions, and our energy. So, a stable platform can be created only using these four components. In other words, if all of these components are stable, only then can we be stable. This four are like legs of a table and even if one is not stable then we won't have a stable platform. If all three are fine and Mind is not fine, what is the use or if body is not healthy what is the use? Once we are aware of these four components, we can have a centre that is not swayed by the turbulences of life. Our body and mind will be in a calm and peaceful state.

Doing any exercise or yoga with awareness has a direct impact on our body and Mind if we do it continuously, both our body and Mind becomes stable. The Emotion is something that needs to be understood and self-knowledge is required for this. Understanding maya is important as it gives us the correct perspective about the world.

Maya

The Sanskrit word 'Maya' is roughly translated as illusion. When we say that the world is a 'Maya', it means seeing the facts of life and not try to find meaning in it, as we will never find the meaning for it. Philosophers or poets may give their meaning to life but it is just their interpretation and it has nothing to do with reality. It is just like if one asks what is the meaning of a flower, a poet may give his interpretation, a lover may give his, but there is no meaning for it. Life is something to be lived and experienced, not to be analysed, just like the beauty of a flower is to be experienced and not analysed.

This interpretation that the world is an illusion has some basis due to the Buddhist philosophers. One section of philosophers did not believe in the external world at all. But the Maya of Vedanta or as per Adi Shankara is neither idealism nor realism, nor is it a theory. It is a simple statement of facts or reality — what we are and what we see around us.

If we look at our own life, we will find that it is a contradiction — a mixture of existence and non-existence. There are problems that a man is not able to solve despite using his intellect although he tries to. He takes few steps forward and a wall appears that seems unbreakable. There are tremendous contradictions in all facets of our life. Reformers raise their voice against corruption and yet, there is corruption going on for ages.

Maya is a statement of the facts of this Universe. We can never find the cause of all our problems because the instrument that is searching for the answers is our mind — that is limited by nature. It cannot go beyond certain limits of time, space, and causation. When the Vedas proclaim — "This world has no existence." What is meant by that? It means that it has no absolute existence on its own. It exists only in relation to my mind, your mind, and to the mind of the every individual in the world. We see this world with our five senses but if we had another sense, a sense that can perceive the magnetic waves, we would see something more. If we had yet another sense, it would appear as something still more different. So, what we perceive as the world has no real existence; it is not something unchangeable, immovable, infinite existence. At the same time it cannot be called non-existence. Seeing that it exists, we need to live and work in and through it. It is a mixture of existence and non-existence.

As a person becomes old and sees death around him, the human mind asks the basic philosophical question, "The whole world is going towards death; everything dies. All our progress, vanities, reforms, luxuries, fame, wealth, knowledge have one end — death. Is that all that is certain?"

Death is the end of life, of the body, of wealth, power and fame. Priests and sinners die, emperors and beggars die. They are all going to die and yet there is a tremendous clinging to life as it exists. Somehow, we do not know why all of us cling to life and why we cannot give it up. This is Maya.

Maya is a statement of the facts of this universe and of how it is going on. People generally get frightened when things like 'death' are told to them. But we must be bold and seek the truth. It is only then that we can find the remedy.

Life by its nature is full of contradictions. There is both good and bad in this world and this has been the way for hundreds of years. We all struggle for happiness, but as soon as we get a little happiness on one side, there is unhappiness on the other side. If we try to increase our happiness, our miseries also increase. There are people who say that we know the world is not perfect but let us ignore it and make ourselves happy. But they are just like a fox who puts his head in a hole when hunted by dogs.

There is not one thing in this world of ours that we can label as good and good alone, and there is not one thing that we can label as bad and bad alone. The very same technology or culture that appears to be good now may appear to be bad tomorrow. The same thing that produces misery in one, may produce happiness in another. The great secret revealed by this understanding is that good and bad are not cut-and-dried, separate existences. They are not black and white. So, a question may be asked — If there is no good and bad, what is the point of doing only good? Why not just enjoy the time that we have?

The entire Western culture is based on ambition and desire. There is nothing wrong with it but they are making a mistake, a tremendous, illogical mistake. They are equating life with only pleasure that can be got through senses. Then, what is the difference between humans and animals? Individuals who have made a positive impact on society didn't live a life based only on seeking pleasure as the ultimate aim. Life has to mean something more than just pleasure perceived through our senses. Our feelings, thoughts, and aspirations are all part and parcel of our life. The struggle towards freedom, ideals, towards perfection, are some of the most important components of what we call life.

We must do our part because that is the only way of getting out of this life of contradiction. Every one of us finds out sooner than later in our lives that doing good for others is the only way to make ourselves happy.

Cause and effect are all Maya. There is no such thing as clear-cut cause and effect — because if we change the present moment then the entire karmic cycle is broken. We can lower our intellect to let any allegory pass through our mind without questioning the connection. We can develop a love of imagery and beautiful poetry and enjoy all mythologies as poetry but not question it using our intellect. We may come to mythology with ideas of history and reasoning. We may let it flow as a current through our mind, let it be whirled as a candle before our eyes without asking — who holds the candle. When we don't analyse the holder, we will get the circle; the residuum of truth will remain in our mind.

God and Religion

With the advancement of religion came ethical ideas. There arose a certain sense in man — the voice of God or voice of conscience. It was the result of past education. It was called by different names in different languages and nations. The effect was that it had a checking power on the natural impulses or senses of man. He was no longer the brute that his ancestor was.

There is one thought in our minds which says indulge in all the pleasures through senses, and there is another voice in our mind which says, do not. Our mind is always struggling to get outside through the channels of the senses, ever-expanding, always unsatisfied with whatever it possesses. It is always looking for more. Behind that, although thin and weak, there is an infinitely small voice that says, do not go outside. The two beautiful Sanskrit words for these phenomena are 'Pravritti' and 'Nivritti'.

PRAVRITTI means to live in this world performing our family duties, making our living. All our actions are primarily directed towards the external world.

NIVRITTI, on the other hand, is the path of 'turning back' or 'looking inside'. It is the path of turning within, towards spiritual contemplation and placing truth and freedom at the centre of our existence, after fulfilling our familial and professional duties.

Fulfilling our responsibilities and duties to our family and society is our basic duty. But some people still feel insecure despite possessing all the wealth — one house after another, one new thing after another are constantly bought and accumulated. These are clear signs that the inner Self has still not had enough. Despite all the disappointments and failures, their mind has not realized the fact that the external world cannot give them joy or bliss.

For as long as we live in 'Pravritti', our mind is focused mainly on worldly things, pleasure and wealth. If we look at our life, initially, school and education occupy our thoughts, then profession and family. Finally, in old age, we worry about our health and our inheritance.

Religion begins with circling inward or going inside us, which is nothing but understanding our minds. Religion and spirituality begin with this 'do not indulge', as our mind will always seek pleasure. When this checking of our senses is not there, spirituality has not begun.

Once these ideas of religion came, a glimpse of something higher and more ethical, dawned upon the intellect of mankind. The God to be worshipped was no more a simple symbol of power. There was something more required than just that. He was also an ethical God, who loved mankind and did good for mankind. But the idea of a personal God still remained. This increased his ethical significance and also his power. He became the benevolent protector and Almighty. But if God is an ethical person with great powers, then the question arose, why are people suffering?

So, this concept of personal God could not be accepted. The God of Heaven became the God within this temple of the body, and the God dwelling in the temple of the body became the temple itself, the soul.

But some men who call themselves practical men advocated that religion is a restriction on their freedom. They said that we must make the most of it and forget about God and religion. They said that they knew this is a very bad world and it stinks, but we can make the best of it. This in plain language means that "we must get used to the smell and live a hypocritical life, a life of continuous fraud, being insensitive to things around us. As long as I am fine. If others are suffering, it is because of their Karma or they are plain lazy". This is what is called practical life.

Those that are satisfied with this patchwork ideology will never come to religion. Spirituality begins with a tremendous dissatisfaction with the present state of things, with our lives, and hatred, intense hatred for this patching up of life, an unbounded disgust for fraud and lies of this society.

Those alone can be spiritual who dare to say, as the mighty Buddha once said when this idea of being practical appeared before him that it was nonsense. He said that death is better than a vegetating, ignorant life. "It is better to die on the battlefield seeking truth than to live a life of defeat."

When the temptation comes to give up this search for truth and go back to the world and live the old life of fraud, calling things by wrong names, telling lies to oneself and to everybody, we should realize that there is something in us that won't get satisfied by limited things be it money or power. The mind will never get satisfied with it; it will always ask for more. Essentially, what it is seeking is something not limited. It is seeking the unlimited because the entity which is seeking itself through the mind is unlimited by its own nature. What it wants, is to be complete and whole again.

Self

There is our mind or ego and there is self in us. "I am angry and I have decided not to be angry" — the part of the mind that has decided not to become angry is not the one that had got angry. There is no meeting. The part of the mind that had got angry will again become angry and the part of the mind which had condemned it, will once again condemn it. The mind thrives on fragments and the ego creates a false sense of 'becoming'.

Self is something total and integrated and it is based on the platform of awareness. The self inside us tries to express itself through the mind and is not satisfied by limited things. What the self wants is something not bound by the physicality of the world but something finer. Since the mind is the only device through which it can express itself, it can look only at the known things. Later, when the mind realizes that everything in the external world is limited by our senses and the unlimited is something beyond the limitations of our senses, the mind will automatically choose to close all its senses, as senses are outbound.

That idea of freedom that the self has perceived was correct, but the mind had projected it outside us. This is because the mind could only perceive things outside us and that was our mistake. The thing that was trying to express itself through the mind was something unlimited. Hence, there will be a time when all of us will realize that this mad rush for things outside is not going to give us either peace or happiness; it can only give us conflict.

It was our Self, expressing itself, trying to reach to its source, which is the un-limitedness or totality. Freedom is our nature and Maya or Nature can never bind us. Nature never has power over us. When a man takes this stand, he is definitely on the way to finding the truth; he is on the way to God. God, who is not up in heaven but a God who is inside us.

Chapter 3 Self Knowledge

To know oneself is the beginning of wisdom. We may have come across many scholars well versed and knowledgeable in scriptures without any real character or virtue. The reason for this is — they have only an intellectual understanding of the scriptures and have no real experience or realization about it. The realization of Shankara, Jesus, Kabir or Krishna cannot be our realization. We have to start from our center, not from the realization of others. Adi Shankara may say "I am Brahman" or "I am God". This may be his realization but if that is not in our experience then repeating the same does not make us Shankara or a realized soul. It just makes us a parrot.

Knowing oneself

So, how does one know oneself? Can we understand ourselves using a book or what others say about us? Or can we know ourselves through self-introspection?
For a real understanding of the mind, we need to touch an element that is finer than the mind. Just as we need a key that is smaller than the lock to open a lock, we need energy that is subtler than the mind. For this, we need to touch the Pure Consciousness or the intelligent part of the mind. Pure consciousness is something that can only be

experienced. Since it is subtler than the mind, it cannot be contained in our memory and hence cannot be analyzed using the mind. The mind can only experience it, not analyze it. This is the reason all the scholars and priests, despite their bookish knowledge, live in their own world without any touch of the reality of life.

A person asked Hui-Neng how to know oneself. Hui-Neng replied, "What is the problem? You are alive and you are conscious that you are alive, so why are you not aware of who you are?"

The question is not "How to know oneself" but to understand what is the barrier that prevents one from understanding themselves. If we can understand the barrier that stops us from understanding ourselves, then the barrier can be dissolved very easily. The real question is not the ways or techniques to know oneself but to realize how we are missing the obvious reality, the basic truth which is so near us. What is preventing us from knowing " Who am I "?

We must have created a wall or a barrier, so nothing positive needs to be done. Anything done by our minds will only strengthen the wall. We just need to understand the nature of the barrier or wall. When the entire universe is going perfectly well without any problem and life is working for us, where is the problem? The problem is a single thought that can hijack our entire consciousness and restrict the 'me' to a limited self. We live in dreams and these dreams become the barrier. Reality is not a dream. It is there all the time and we are surrounded by it. The only reason we miss it is because we are dreaming. When we dream, reality is distorted.

Self-knowledge is the most difficult thing — not because it requires effort or hardship, but because we are afraid to know about ourselves. Everyone fears about the content of their subconsciousness. If we notice, we can observe everybody trying to escape from themselves. This fear has to be understood. Without this understanding, we will continuously avoid and deceive ourselves. On one hand, we will try to know ourselves and on the other hand, we will create all sorts of hindrances so that we cannot know. Consciously we may think, "I would like to know myself," but in the unconscious which is bigger, stronger, and more powerful than the conscious, we will avoid self-knowledge. So, the fear has to be understood. Why are we afraid? One thing is that if we penetrate within ourselves, our image will break. We have created an image about ourselves and have invested a lot in it. We would like to maintain that image and the basic fear is what if that is not true and the image that we have created in the world happens to be a fake. Then, our whole past will mean nothing because it has been like a dream. We have invested so much in that image and we have lived for it, and to know that it has been a false phenomenon would hurt, and our whole life would have been wasted. It is like investing our whole life in a political ideology that we believe is true and after decades of investing and putting energy and effort, we suddenly realize that it was a wrong ideology and what we believed and stood for was just a façade and we have been used by a cunning politician to serve his purpose.

It would mean whatsoever life we have been living has been a pseudo-life — not authentic. We have never loved but just pretended to love. Realising this how can we encounter ourselves? Because then we will come to know that the whole thing has been a pretense — not only have we pretended that we love, we have also pretended that we are happy when we love. In the end, we have deceived nobody else but ourselves. Now, when we look back and look within, fear grips us.

All the time, we have been thinking and told by society that we are something unique and special. So, most of us like to think of ourselves as extraordinary, something special, 'the chosen one'. But if we truly look at ourselves, we will come to know that there is nothing to be egoistic about. Then, where will the ego stand? It will crumble and turn to dust.

Fear exists so we do not look at ourselves. In not looking, we can go on creating dreams and images about ourselves. It is very easy and cheap to create an image but it is very difficult and hard to be something real. One always chooses the cheapest and we have chosen the cheapest. To look at it now is difficult.

Relationships are mirrors

All opinions and conclusions that we have about ourselves may not be true. It cannot be just plain self-deception, as it is in the case of many. So, the only way we can know ourselves is through a relationship. How we behave in a relationship is what one truly is, not what we think we are. My self-image could be based on my desire and not reality. If we can easily and effortlessly interact with hundreds of people without any hindrance then it means our content is free from conflict.

The moment we feel a sense of uneasiness in any relationship, it means that our mind which was flowing freely has hit a block or 'knot'. The relationship is a mirror where one can see himself as one truly is and self-knowledge is possible, provided we do not condemn what we see in it.

For this, the person should be genuinely interested in knowing himself. When a person understands himself and does not run away from it either by denying it or justifying, what they see in the mirror reveals the truth about themselves. This truth will free the person. This leads to freedom. Freedom from all the negative emotions like fear, anger, envy, and jealousy.

Along with interest and curiosity, one should also not have been conditioned by the morality of the world. The morality of the church is not true morality. It is being done only to create fear and control the people, and hence there is no virtue in it. If we are conditioned by what good and bad is based on a religious book, however great it may be, we can never really understand ourselves. We would attach ourselves to what the book says as good and distance ourselves from the bad and hence, live in self-deception.

If the book says indulging in a particular habit is bad or sinful, it will make us feel guilty and sinners. This will create conflict in our minds. A mind which is not peaceful or calm can never understand the truth. The truth is, if we just look at the act without any judgment, then we will go to the root of that problem. For this, we need to be free from the authority of religion, church, and the Holy Book. Without any relationship, one can just isolate himself and come to any conclusion about himself. This is what most of us do. But when we enter into the relationship, we find that we don't have the virtues that we imagined we had and the reality hits us. Instead of being aware of the reality of that situation, we do not like what we see in ourselves and try to blame others.

If there is any sense of uneasiness in a relationship, the only person responsible can be ourselves because whatever may be the external situation, (not physical but psychological) how we choose to react should be in our control. Others cannot choose how we react. If they can make us react, then it simply means that we are not a free person, as the external situation determines who we are. If we are happy when the situation is pleasant and when the situation becomes unpleasant, we are not so happy, it means that we don't have any individuality and we depend on the environment to make us happy.

This does not mean we suppress our emotions. It just means that we should be aware of the situation and in this awareness, we can observe our reaction. Once we are aware of that reaction, we understand ourselves. But for this understanding to happen, we should not judge ourselves. This understanding can come only when our mind is silent and intelligence operates.

Freedom from authority

The churches or any other religions have always said, "Give your life to us, we will direct it, shape it and tell you what to do. Do this, follow the savior, follow the church and you will have peace and happiness". On the contrary, churches have started terrible wars. Religions have brought division of humanity through their books and their interpretation of God. This has created a fragmentation of the entire humanity based on religion.

This division has been perpetuated by the authority of religion for gaining control over the people and thus maintaining their power and authority. So, the question is not about freedom from a particular authority, the authority of the Church, the authority of politicians, but the whole conceptual acceptance of authority.

Why do we accept authority? Our minds feel secure when we have the blessing of the Church or the Pope. It is fear that makes us accept authority. Our mind is always looking for security. In case of uncertainty, it always looks for authority either through religion or book to guide us. The truth is, nothing in life is ever secure and that makes our minds always feel insecure about the future. The future is never certain and this creates fear in our minds and makes us conform to authority.

But this obedience is born of fear: fear of going wrong, of acting independently, of not being secure, of not being part of the community, of standing alone, of making a mistake. So, it is fear that breeds authority. Everyone wants to live in a respected, accepted way which the society has established.

Self-knowledge and Life

Without knowing oneself, not partially but fully, or integrally, it is not possible to think right, and therefore act right. Without self-knowledge, there cannot be complete, integrated action. There can only be partial action. When there is no self-knowledge, it will invariably lead to conflict and misery.

To understand the problems of life completely or the problem of relationships, we must understand ourselves first, and we can understand ourselves only in relationship, and that is action. There is action only when we understand a relationship — a relationship not only with people and ideas but also with things and nature.

Without self-knowledge, life will be contradictory, painful, and a constant source of conflict. So, to understand this process of life, we have to understand the significance of our own thoughts and feelings. This is why self-knowledge is very important.

Knowledge about Self

Science means knowledge. If something is unknowable, science will not approve of it. Science means that which can be known and measured. It cannot fall into absurdities. For science, the very word self-knowledge is absurd as there is no self as per science. But in religion, it has meaning because there is another dimension of knowing.

If a lamp is burning in a dark room, then everything in the room is known through the light from the lamp. The lamp is also known by its own light. Everything else chairs, furniture, walls, paintings on the walls are known through the light from the lamp. But through 'what' is the light itself known?

The knowledge of the furniture depends on the light but the knowledge of the light itself doesn't depend on the chair. If we remove all the furniture from the room and make it empty, even then the light will still be light. There will be nothing to reveal — no furniture, no chairs, no painting, but even then, the light will go on revealing itself. That revelation of the light is self-revelation. This is the case with the inner self. There is a difference between matter and consciousness. Consciousness is self-revealing; it knows itself whereas matter has to be known through someone else. This is the basic difference between matter and consciousness. If there is no conscious being, then matter cannot be revealed; it needs someone's consciousness so that it can be revealed.

When a Yogi goes to a forest, the trees are revealed. Now, it is not a mute existence. Through the Yogi, the tree and nature have become assertive. Everything around the Yogi becomes alive in a new meaning. The Yogi has become a source of revelation. Everything around him becomes alive due to his consciousness. Hence, the deeper our consciousness, the deeper we reveal existence.

When a Buddha is born, the whole existence celebrates in him because of such a deep consciousness. All that is hidden in matter becomes manifest. Although it was never known before, by the mere presence of an enlightened person, the whole existence around him is enlightened. Everything becomes alive and feels through him. Consciousness reveals others, but there is no need to reveal it for another consciousness. It is self-revelatory.

Chapter 4 Mind

In modern medicine and modern science, there is a tendency to identify the mind as a function of the brain and the consciousness as a function of the mind. When there is a problem in the mind, the source of the problem is seen as an imbalance in the brain and hence there is a tendency to treat the brain chemically, making well-being a good chemistry of the brain.

BRAIN (Physical) -> MIND (physiological) ->CONSCIOUNESS (Individual Self)

This has led to the belief in western society that nobody is individually responsible for their emotions or state of mind and what one needs to do is fix the brain. It is believed that we can feel better by altering and changing the chemistry of the brain through drugs. For example, depression is said to be the result of having too little serotonin in the brain and to fix it, we need a shot of serotonin.

Hence, huge money is spent in finding the right chemical which will create a sense of well-being and happiness. There are several medications available that claim to work by changing the levels of certain brain chemicals. These drugs alter the levels of neurotransmitters like dopamine, noradrenaline, serotonin, or norepinephrine. Some work in a combination of two or more of these chemicals.

In the yogic system, not much importance is attached to the brain. The brain is just part of the body like the heart, kidney or liver. The brain is a physical object that can be seen with the eyes, can be photographed, or operated in surgery. The mind, on the other hand, is not a physical object. It cannot be seen with the eyes, nor can it be photographed, or cut by surgery.

The brain therefore, unlike the mind, is simply a part of the body. There is nothing within the body that can be identified as being our mind because our body and mind are different entities. For example, sometimes when our body is relaxed and immobile, our mind can be very busy, moving from one subject to another. This indicates that our body and mind are not the same entity.

What is the Mind

In the yogic system, the mind is referred to as 'chitta'. Happiness or bliss happens when the thoughts or waves in the 'chitta' or lake come to rest.

The entire yogic philosophy is built around emptying the contents of the mind so that it does not create suffering. The turbulence of the mind indicates thoughts. More turbulence means more thoughts which translates to an individual becoming less clear and more emotional.

Definition of Yoga is — "yogash chitta vritti nirodha". This means — Yoga is nothing but stopping (nirodha) the spread (vritti) of waves of the mind (chitta).

Just like ripples are caused when we throw a stone into a lake, thoughts are caused when our minds react to the situation from the outside. Thoughts are 'vritti' in the lake called 'chitta'. More the thoughts, less clearly one can see.

The entire yogic science is based on stopping or limiting the thoughts. Different yoga systems give different steps to stop these waves or 'vritti'.

'Becoming' is modification of our mind and the amount of modification of thoughts determines the consciousness level of mind. The less the number of thoughts, the more aware a person becomes of the situation.

When someone blames or criticizes us, this causes a modification in our mind (chitta) and the mind becomes agitated. It is just like a stone thrown in a lake causes turbulence in the water. We identify ourselves with that particular thought or modification and we become or take the shape of that thought. The thought creates in us the ego. Ego being a fragment of the whole will never be able to address the problem fully, as we won't be able to perceive the reality of that situation. We perceive it based on our thoughts which come from our memory. Since memory is limited, the entity born out of that thought is nothing but our personal self, or 'ahankara', or ego, which is also limited or fragmented by nature.

For example, take an oyster. We know how pearls are made. A grain of sand gets inside the oyster shell and begins to irritate it. The oyster creates a sort of enamel around the sand particle and this makes the pearl. This whole universe is our own enamel, so to say, and the real universe is the grain of sand. An ordinary man will never understand the reality, because when he tries to, he sees only his own enamel or conclusions based on his past understanding. These are nothing but his experiences from the past. He will not able to see the current reality, as the problems are always new and his experience is from the past. One cannot drive a car by looking at a rear-view mirror. To understand a problem, we just need to be aware and the solution will emerge from the problem itself. We don't have to formulate a solution.

We end up being a prisoner of our memory. Our thoughts keep the mind occupied with its own projections and we are not able to perceive life in its pure or pristine form. All our perception of life is contaminated by our memory. This memory contains a pattern of thought based on our past experience and that is karma. When we say that all that is happening is karma, it means that our mind is limited by the pattern of our own experience. To be free of karma means our mind is in the present and it is acting based on the reality of the situation and not from the old pattern in the memory.

Hence, our karma or impressions from the past is the root cause for all our suffering and we are not able to handle any crises completely. What we experience in life is nothing but our own projections and for us to experience life fully, we need to change our quality of mind and make it more conscious. This is done not by altering chemicals in our brain but by understanding our minds.

For most of us, just one thought is enough to cause disturbance and ruin an otherwise perfect day. Just thinking about a job to be done the next day is enough to make our mind stressed or anxious.

The mind (Chitta) keeps moving like air and it is difficult to control our thoughts. When the mind or Chitta is totally silent, there is no identification with memory, either past or future, when one is completely aware, then intelligence will shine through that mind. It is like looking at a still lake and being able to see the bottom of the lake. At the bottom of that lake, we find our own image.

Intelligence or chit (not Chitta) need not be created, as it is something that already exists within all. All one has to do is stop these waves and what shines through the mind is nothing but pure intelligence.

Dimensions of the Mind

Mind (Chitta) is nothing but a collection of imprints (Samskaras). Chit (Intelligence) is different from Chitta which represents the mind. Our personality is nothing but a bundle of habits based on our likes and dislikes. All our actions are based on our desires arising from our contact with different objects. The mind consists of different dimensions:

1.   Buddhi (Intellect)

2.   Manas (Memory)

3.   Ahankara (Ego)

4.   Chit (Pure intelligence or Consciousness)

These are 'Vritti-bhedas' or functional aspects of the mind. Buddhi or Intellect: Intellect is nothing but the knowledge acquired through books, education, society and from our own experience of life. The nature of intellect is to discriminate based on measurement and comparison. Buddhi will always compare two things or dissect a thing into parts and try to make meaning out of it.
If you give a flower to a scientist and ask him to find the source of the perfume, he will first dissect the flower and individually analyze each part under a microscope. He will analyze minute parts of the flower trying to find the source of the perfume but will miss the whole flower.

Our entire education system does nothing but sharpens the intellect of the student which involves gathering knowledge or information through books, memorizing it, and repeating it. Nothing wrong with knowledge. It is important and required in our daily work or our profession. A spaceship that goes to the moon consists of thousands of parts and needs skilled, technical people with good knowledge in different branches of sciences.

Intellect is one aspect of the Mind — a useful one too, but only things which are material and physical can be dissected and understood. Those that are not physical like — life or people are beyond the capability of intellect. The reason is that intellect is based on knowledge or memory and knowledge is static or limited at any specific point in time. So, intellect can make sound assumptions based on facts that will appear to be correct at that particular point of time. Later, when the knowledge of those subjects increases, the assumptions also change.

Intellect is a tool that is designed for our survival or basic function of life. It is like a knife that can only dissect things. It is limited because for it to operate, it needs memory. 'Buddhi' cannot function without memory. Memory, as everyone knows, may consist of knowledge based on facts but when it comes to people and life situations, it is not facts but opinions based on their own experience. This opinion is subject to change with time.

Opinions about people are not something static. People and life are dynamic and ever-changing. But memory keeps a snapshot of people based on experience, which is static and later intellect uses that past memory to judge the present situation. Hence, our entire conclusion will be mostly based on the first snapshot of that person. This is usually taken by the mind when the mind feels pleasure or feels threatened. Having a final conclusion about anything is bound to be wrong. Life is something that needs to be experienced moment to moment and cannot be summed up.

Seeing or perceiving life as wholesome is beyond the capabilities of intellect as it does all the processing based on memory. Hence, its conclusion is limited or fragmented. Buddhi or intellect's main function is survival. Survival is vital for the human race to continue. For survival, memory is important as it tells us which fruit is good and which one is poisonous and also helps to learn from past mistakes.

The entire humanity is not suffering their life but their memory or their karma. Intellect (Buddhi) like a sharp knife starts dissecting people and situations, trying to resolve the problems they face in life. But with people, you need to be inclusive to understand them and this inclusive nature is not of the Buddhi but of love.

Manas — a silo of memory

Mana means memory. All the things captured by our senses are stored in Manas. All our experience is stored in Manas. Without Manas, the human race could not have survived. The only reason we are still around is because of the wonderful faculty we have called Manas.

Manas can also become the source of major suffering, as we can recollect the hurt that we had 10 years ago and still feel the pain now. Because of Manas, we are never able to live in the present moment. Thoughts always arise from Manas and are always of the past. That thought from the past is projected into the future and we start experiencing things that are yet to happen. For example, if we had a bad experience with a person last year and are going to meet the same person tomorrow, our Manas will project the past into the future and come up with all kinds of worst scenarios. But in reality, when we meet the person and are open-minded, we may find that the person has changed over that period.

Whatever be the IQ of an individual, if the memory or knowledge is wiped out from a person, he will no longer look smart. But that does not mean that person is not conscious, as consciousness does not depend on memory or knowledge. From school days, people have been conditioned to gather knowledge because a person with knowledge was considered to be intelligent. Knowledge or information makes an individual look very smart but having only knowledge without intelligence and using it intellectually without any awareness of reality, makes one miss the exuberance or joy of life, and end up making the mind mechanical.

Memory is all over the body and specifically in the genetic center. We will see more about this in later chapters. The human body carries the memory of everything that has happened from the start of human life that took form on this planet. Hence, it becomes important to understand memory. If the mind can use memory when required and un-clutch from it when not required, then the memory becomes a source of strength and clarity.

Freedom basically means we have a choice about when to use memory and when not to use it. If we don't have that freedom, then our life is not in our hands and is something that happens automatically without our control. This is nothing but Karma. Karma is nothing but actions performed under the influence of memory. All the tendencies that we have is based on our conditioning and memory imprints. If we are free from that tendency, then we are free from our karma and our actions would be based on intelligence.

Memory is a tremendous possibility. But memory is also a limitation and a boundary, as our thinking is limited by what we know, and what we know is not complete. So, fundamentally the mind would not be able to solve any issues other than technical and work problems that require memory and application of the information we already possess.

Being in the present, being aware reduces the influence of memory. It also gives rest to our restless minds. Our efficiency grows, as there is attention that does not require effort.

So how does the Buddhi or intellect choose which imprint to pick from the memory? There might be different memories. There is a logic used by the intellect in picking one memory while ignoring others. For example, a friend might have helped us many times and this is recorded in memory. On a couple of occasions, he might not have us helped due to some reasons. Since the fundamental purpose of intellect or Buddhi is survival, it will always pick the memory associated with fear or pleasure, which is usually an unpleasant one, one of not helping. This is done by the intellect because it finds those memories relevant for survival with the basic intention of avoiding that situation in the future. This is the reason the mind comes up with the worst-case scenario, as it has been stored by the mind for survival purposes.

Ahankara or identification with the ego

When a child is born, it has a Self but not ego. When a child is born, it is born with consciousness but it is not aware of its consciousness. The child first becomes aware of his mother, then slowly becomes aware of his body, and then becomes aware of the objects around him. He realizes that he is separate from the objects around him and this creates a feeling of separation. This leads to the child identifying himself with his body and the ego is born.

As a child, the ego identifies itself with the body but later when the child grows up, his education conditions him with a personality. He identifies himself with nation, religion, language or profession as without any identification he feels empty or powerless.

As the child grows into a man, he realizes the emptiness and the ego creates a dream to hide this emptiness. The ego creates a dream that someday he will become powerful. In Present he feels powerless, impotent, inferior, but in the dream, he feels he will become powerful.

We can realize this if we are aware of our thoughts. We sometimes start daydreaming. We dream of becoming the emperor of the whole world or the president of the United States and immediately start enjoying it. Everybody looks at us. We become the focal point of everyone's attention. Even a dream about that gives us exhilaration and intoxication. When the mind thinks of power, it contemplates power but those are simply dreams and nothing else. Dreams are woven just to hide the inner emptiness within us. But dreams cannot hide reality. The reality is — with a bigger house and a bigger bank balance, we will actually feel more impotent and powerless. In the east, all religions have preached ego-lessness. So, in the east, everybody is against the ego from the very beginning. Because of this anti-ego attitude, the ego never becomes strong. It never comes to a point of developing a strong personality that can do something in this world. People who could not undergo hardship simply took to religion to avoid responsibility towards the family and the society. So, in the east, it is impossible or difficult to dissolve the ego.

In the west, the entire western tradition of religion and psychology persuades people to have strong egos because unless one has a strong ego, how can one survive in this competitive world? Life is a struggle. If we are egoless or without any personality, we will be destroyed. Who will resist? Who will fight? Who will compete? Life is a continuous competition. Western psychology says: develop the ego and be strong in it.

In the west, it is very easy to dissolve the ego. So, whenever a western seeker reaches an understanding that ego is a pseudo entity, he can easily dissolve it. He can dissolve it more easily than any eastern seeker. The contradiction is that in the west ego is taught while in the east ego-less is preached. But in the west, it is easy to dissolve the ego, while in the east, it is very difficult.

Ego is the link between two diametrically opposite natures we have. If we notice, we will criticize somebody, and later we will also defend his action. The human mind is divided and split and ego exists only when we are divided, as we need ego to make connections between the divided parts of our being. We need this link otherwise we will fall apart. Ego is the link between two diametrically opposite parts. It is the rope that binds them together. But once we are together we don't need the ego as the ego is a tension.

There is no need to be clever and cunning with the ego. We just have to be alert, aware, and watchful. Just look at it to see what it is – whether it exists or not. All those who have looked at it have found without exception that it is not there. It is there only when one is unaware; the moment we pay attention to it — it is not there.

The purpose of the ego is to sustain its existence as long as possible. It wants endless pleasures and wants to avoid pain. When we are controlled by our ego, essentially, we act and behave in the world with this identity. All our emotions and impulses are largely driven by this ego. In other words, the thought of pleasure makes us happy. The thought of the loss of that pleasure makes us worried and fearful. This cycle of thoughts goes on inside the ego even when nothing is happening in the real world.

Perfection is a disease that has come from the west and perfection is possible in the case of the external world of machines, that is the reason the western civilization has advanced much in the external world but in the case of the inner world, there is only totality or whole which is called "Purnam" in Sanskrit.

God is whole, not perfect, and out of God, only totality is possible. We come as a whole, we come with the signature of God. The perfectionist is neurotic. Anybody who wants to be perfect in any way will become neurotic. Neurosis is based on the idea of perfection -- because we can never be perfect but we can become whole by just including everyone. They don't have to be perfect being just being inclusiveness will make us whole.

Only this total movement can bring us to a realization where ego cannot exist. Ego can be found with intellect, it can be found with feeling -- but never with our total being.

It can be found with intellect because intellect has no center of its own. It will not allow the center of the total to come into operation, so the intellect has to create its own center. It becomes the ego. The feeling will not allow the total, so feeling has its own center -- it becomes the ego.

With feeling or with intellect, the ego is bound to be there. Only with totality is there no ego. If we are and we don't feel any "I", we are total. When we are listening we should listen without "I" in us. And this is possible if we are just curious and without any judgment. Ears are there, a listening process is there, our consciousness is there, but no "I", and then we are total. There is no division without an "I"? Without an ego, how can we be divided? The ego is the division and division means duality and duality is the source for all our conflict.

Chit or Pure intelligence

This is the dimension of intelligence that is unsullied by memory. It is free of memory, free from the conditioning of society, and has not identified itself with anything. This intelligence alone can lead one to the source of creation itself. Once our mind touches 'chit', we touch the source of creation itself.

Intelligence as per yogic science is something that exists in everyone. The reason it is not fully exhibited is because it is covered by imprints or karma. Chit or consciousness is something inherent and omnipresent in all humans, and how much intelligence is present depends on the quality of the mind or the awareness of the mind. The less aware one is, which is more the waves or thoughts, the less the consciousness exhibited. If the mind (Chitta) is totally silent, it means one is fully aware — one is an enlightened person.

When all thoughts in our mind come to naught, then what is shining through our mind is nothing but pure intelligence. Different religions have called it by different names such as Brahman or God. In that state, there is no sense of 'I', as the mind is free from all memory, and the mind does not take any shape in the form of a name and form. There are no 'vrittis' (vibrations) and hence no ego.

Chit Shakti is about touching that dimension of our mind that is pure intelligence — unsullied by memory, unsullied by identification, unsullied by judgment. It is beyond ahankara, beyond buddhi, beyond judgment, beyond divisions. It is simply there, just like the intelligence of existence that makes everything happen. If we can access this, we do not have to worry about any security and will be free from all our fear and conflicts. The only way to access this intelligence is through meditation.

Different states of consciousness

Every manifestation, appearance, or action in the universe is a part of Nature. The nature and life force which is called consciousness starts in man from the limited sphere and extends its dimension step by step, stage by stage, towards a further understanding of its own existence and realization of Godliness in oneself.

The consciousness is limited by our mind, as the mind operates through its senses and senses are limited. Hence, when we turn to the external world, we are limited by our senses. But when we enter into our internal space with awareness or meditation, we discover a different level of consciousness.

There are there 3 levels of Consciousness above the personal self and 3 levels of unconsciousness under it:

3. Cosmic Conscious mind — one with the whole of existence. It is Samadhi. There are no questions. All questions are dissolved. Eternally blissful experience, brahman, or Godliness.
2. Super Conscious mind — Experience one consciousness from the beginning
1. No Mind — awareness is present and no thoughts exist in the mind

Conscious mind — Personal self

1. Unconscious Mind
2. Collective Unconscious Mind
3. Cosmic Unconscious Mind

The unconscious mind is nine times bigger than the conscious mind and has memories of our past lives. In our collective unconscious mind, we have memories of our past lives as animals and birds. Below the collective unconscious mind, there is the cosmic unconscious where we have memories of being trees and stones. Western phycologists were interested in the domain below the conscious mind while eastern mystics were interested in the higher domain. Sigmund Freud was the first to bring this idea out that man has a great unconscious hidden in him, Jung, went a little further, a little deeper, and discovered the collective unconscious. Behind the individual unconscious, there is a collective unconscious.

Just as Freud and Jung opened the dimension below the conscious, Sri Aurobindo opened the dimension above the conscious. That dimensions can be attained only through meditation. When our ordinary conscious mind is added to meditation, it becomes the real conscious mind. Beyond the real conscious mind is the superconscious mind.

The only way is to go a little higher than the conscious mind, where society has not conditioned anything, and which is absolutely pure and innocent is the Superconsciousness. The superconscious is more powerful than the conscious; and it is innocent, as innocent as the unconscious and the difference between them is that the unconscious is dark, and the superconscious is alert, full of light. It can see things in its own light, it does not need any borrowed insights.

So the only possibility to create a transformation is to bring the superconscious in. Then the conscious mind cannot do anything. The superconscious mind can relieve the conscious mind of its conditionings. It can allow the unconscious mind to release, through the conscious, all its repressed contents. And the miracle is that the moment the unconscious mind has released all its contents, it loses darkness, it is no longer unconscious. Then you have a great energy that is conscious.

Now all three parts of our mind, unconscious, conscious, and superconscious have become one. And the dominant factor will remain the superconscious.

Being intelligent is our natural state but most of us are not that because of our genetic center, memory imprints, or samskaras. It is something that keeps on generating waves (thoughts) and we identify ourselves with that. Hence, meditation is one way by which we simply witness our thoughts. The intellect can never understand meditation, as being silent cannot be measured.

Mind and Energy

According to Vethathiri Maharishi, "Lifeforce particles in their self-rotator whirling movement produce biomagnetic waves. These waves function as through our senses. When biomagnetic waves pass through the brain, it functions as the mind".

The mind is the collection of biomagnetic waves which has the self-transforming capability and speed. The speed or the mental frequency can be measured as cycles per second. EEG is an apparatus that records this in the form of a drawing of the electrical activity of the brain. Scientists using EEG have discovered that mental frequency level is from 1 to 40 cycles per second (CPS).

When the mind functions through the five senses, the mind is at different frequencies based on the state of its consciousness. These states are known as — 'Jagrata' or waking, 'Svapna' or dreaming, 'Sushupti' or deep sleep, and 'Turiya'.

Their frequencies are:

Beta (14 to 40 CPS)— Awake, Normal alert,

Conscious (Jagrata) Alpha (9 to 13 CPS) — Relaxed, Calm, Lucid, Not thinking

Theta (4 to 8 CPS) — Deep relaxation, Meditation, Mental imagery (Svapna)

Delta (1 to 3 CPS) — Deep and Dreamless Sleep (Sushupti)

As the waves of the mind reduce, we move to different levels of consciousness and there is a state called 'turiya', where there are no thoughts but only pure observation with full awareness. This is the state of enlightenment or fulfillment. The whole search and effort of Yoga is attaining this state.

During meditation, the mind which was going 'on and on' nonstop, realizes that there is a state or consciousness level, where it cannot operate. It cannot simply operate because there is no memory. Without it, it cannot evaluate and come to a judgment. So, only random thoughts will come to mind and we just have to witness it without becoming it. Meditation is like sitting in front of a river and just witnessing the water current as it flows.

Meditation is very important, as it is the only way we can reduce our thoughts. When we do that, we understand ourselves as we are, however it is — ugly or beautiful, wicked or mischievous, envious or greedy, without any distortion. This is a virtue.

Meditation is nothing but an effort to reach Turiya state. In this state, there is a complete perception of both the inner and outer. It is a total awakening. There is no darkness left within or without. This state is called by different names in different religions. This is the state experienced by Buddha and is called Samadhi. Here, there is only awareness, not an experience or an experiencer. The criteria of truth are not experienced in past tenses, but that state in which neither the experiencer exists nor is there any experience. It is called 'shoonya' or emptiness or 'turiya' as the mind does not take any form. It can be called a no-mind or simply being aware without the interference of the mind.

Chapter 5 Working of the Mind

The activities of the mind are frighteningly monotonous and mechanical. The mind is a bore and intrinsically enervating, pointless and futile. Its opposing and conflicting desires, its hopes and frustrations, its realities and illusions are enthralling and yet empty. All its activities lead to its own weariness. The mind is ever climbing and ever falling down, ever pursuing one pleasure after another and ever being frustrated, ever gaining and ever losing; and from this weary round of futility, it is ever trying to escape. It tries to escape by becoming, becoming is a process of expansion of the mind through something an object, or an idea.

Becoming — the process of the Mind

This process of becoming causes the mind to become weary and frustrated. The mind then tries to escape through outward activities by indulging in pleasure either through drink, sex, music, or through God and religion. The mind has the power to create an illusion that is vast and complex. These illusions are self-made to escape the boredom and weariness of working in the same office for two decades or doing a job that is meaningless and tiresome. These illusions are self-projected, a form of self-aggrandizement to escape from the present. This illusion is projected into the future creating a sense of pleasure and excitement. The mind can never be in the present. It can be either in the past in the form of regret or in the future.

The content of its consciousness which is nothing but all our experience stored in memory is projected by the mind into the future. It cannot be in the present since no memory is required to be in the present and without memory, our intellect cannot operate.

The Mind always seeks pleasure

Self-forgetfulness is sought within and without. Some turn to religion and others turn to work but there is no means of forgetting the mind. The inner or outward attraction can suppress the mind, but it soon comes up again in a different form, under a different guise because what is suppressed must find a release. What is suppressed goes to the sub-consciousness and will always come back to the conscious mind.

Self-forgetfulness through drink or sex, through worship or music, makes for dependence on the substance and creates a habit. This habit creates a problem when continued over time. The habit becomes behavior, and behavior repeated over time gets into the emotional part of our mind.

If we depend for release, self-forgetfulness, and happiness — on drink or relationships, then they become our problem. Dependence breeds possessiveness, envy, and fear. Fear by itself creates anxiety and we lose our peace. Then, overcoming it becomes our problem. In the search for happiness, we create problems and we get caught in them. We find some happiness in the self-forgetfulness of sex and so we use it to escape the boredom of everyday living. But sex too becomes a problem as the conditioning done by the religions and the Church creates its own set of guilt and conflict.

Happiness sought through something must invariably create conflict, for the means becomes more significant than happiness itself. If I get happiness through the wealth of land, then the land becomes important to me and I must guard it against others. In this struggle, the happiness that I once felt in the value of the land is utterly forgotten, lost, and I am left with the land. In itself, the land has little value but I have given it an extraordinary value because it is the means of my happiness. So, the means become a substitute for happiness.

When the means of my happiness is a living person, then the conflict and confusion, the antagonism, and pain are far greater. If a relationship is based on mere usage or ownership, is there any true relationship, except the most superficial, between the user and the used ? If I use people for my happiness, am I really related to them? A relationship implies communion with another on different levels. Can there be any real communion with another when he is only a tool — a means for my happiness?

Are we not really seeking self-isolation in which we think both of us will be happy by using the other? So, the relationship becomes a source of self-isolation. There is no communion in this process. Communion can exist only where there is no fear. There is fear and pain where there is usage and dependence in a relationship. As nobody can live in isolation, the attempts of the mind to isolate itself will always lead to its own frustration and misery. To escape from this sense of incompletion, we seek completion in ideals, in people, in books, God, sex, and wealth. So, we are back again where we started — in the search for substitutes.

How we regard the problem is of the greatest importance because our attitude and prejudices, our fears and hopes will color it. Choiceless awareness of our approach will bring the right relationship to the problem. The problem is self-created, so there must be self-knowledge. The mind and the problem are one, not two separate processes. 'I am the problem'. Awareness is the silent and choiceless observation of the problem. It is not in trying to find the solution, as trying to find a solution is a subtle attempt to escape from the problem. In this awareness, the problem unravels itself, and thus it is fully and completely understood. It is the truth that frees us from the tendencies of our mind, not our effort. The effort is also part of the same old, cunning mind separating itself from the problem that it has itself created. So, when we realize that any effort will only create another fragmentation of the mind, our mind will automatically become silent, as it has realized that any direction the mind takes is only going to create more problems. Once our mind becomes silent on its own, the truth will enter. We don't have to go to the truth, the truth will come to us.

Mind is conscious only in the beginning

We are conscious in everything just in the beginning and then the unconscious takes over. The unconscious takes charge and the unconscious becomes the master. We can start with any emotion like anger, but we never end it; it is the anger that ends us. We can start anything, but sooner or later, the unconscious takes charge. Our conscious mind is relieved of its duty. Only the beginning is in our hands, never the end and we are not in control of the consequences that follow.

The reason for this is that only a small fragment of the mind is aware. It works just like a starter in the motor. Once we start it, the motor will run continuously. Once we start thinking, we will go deeper and deeper into the subconscious and we may think we are the master. But emotion has taken over us, and we cannot stop once emotion takes over. This is something we can see in our relationships. The moment we start thinking about a past incident, initially, we are in control. Later, the act becomes involuntary and slowly, we will get into the intense feeling. We have no control because the conscious mind is just the upper layer; it is just the surface of the mind and the whole mind is unconscious. We start and the unconscious begins to move in and start its work.

The main function of the Mind is thinking

The mind is always occupied with something. If we just observe ourselves for a few minutes in between our daily activities, we will find the mind always occupied with something. It could be money, health, love, or work, but it is always occupied with something. Intelligence can come only when the mind is silent. So, the question is — how can one make the mind silent?

If we observe, who is asking this question, then we will find that the entity which asks the question is intellect or buddhi, which is also a part of the mind. The buddhi or intellect by its nature is the one asking for methods or steps to become silent. So, it is important to understand the intellect which asks the steps to become silent rather than use will or discipline is given by the intellect to force the mind into obedience.

The mind can never become silent by will, or discipline, or through any process. Any process involves two things — one superior entity which is trying to control another entity. This is duality and will always lead to conflict. Once the mind realizes that the superior entity is also the mind and the entity it is trying to control is also part of the same mind, then this realization will make the mind silent by itself. It also realizes that any movement of the mind in any direction is not going to make it silent.

Can thinking solve our problems

Before we go into what is thinking, it is better to understand if thinking can really solve our problems. If we realize that it does not, then the intellect or buddhi will stop itself from thinking and become silent.

Can thinking dissolve our problems? Of course, in this case, the problem is our psychological problem. We have no conflict when we use our mind in solving math problems or in accounts. Thinking has not solved our problems. The brilliant ones, philosophers, scholars, political leaders have not really solved any of our human problems such as the relationship between us and others, between me and myself.

So far, we have used the mind, the intellect, to help us investigate the problem and through the intellect, we are hoping to find a solution. Can thought ever solve our problems? Is not thought, unless it is in the field of science or technology always self-protecting, self-perpetuating, conditioned, and concerned about oneself? All the activities of the mind are self-centered. Can such thought ever resolve any of the problems which were created by the mind itself? Can the mind, which has created the problems, resolve those things that it has itself brought upon itself?

If we observe more, when we think over a problem, the more we investigate, analyze and discuss it, the more complex it becomes. This is because intellect or buddhi cannot look at the problem comprehensively or wholly. Buddhi or intellect can only dissect information to solve any problem, and when we start dissecting we reach a stage where we get completely lost. Whether it is an atom or the origination of universe, more the data the scientist get more puzzling it becomes as to understand anything we need to be inclusive and not exclusive.

Seeing this incapability of the mind, being aware of the process of our own thinking, and realizing that it actually leads nowhere, we realize that there is a state of intelligence that is not individual. Then, the problem of the relationship of the individual to another individual, of the individual to the society, of the individual to reality, ceases. There is only intelligence, which is neither personal nor impersonal. It is this intelligence alone that can solve our problems whether it is a relationship problem or a problem of the mind. This intelligence does not belong to any individual, as the source of it is not from our memory or manas. It comes into being only when we understand this whole process of thinking, not only at the conscious level, but also at the deeper, hidden levels of consciousness and that is meditation.

Mind and Meditation

To understand any of the problems, we need to have a very quiet, very still mind. It needs a look at the problem without interposing ideas or theories, without any distraction from our past experience or memory. One of our main difficulties is that our thought has become a distraction. When we want to understand or look at a problem, we don't have to think about it, we just need to look at it with complete attention. The moment we begin to think, to have ideas, opinions about it, we are already in a state of distraction. So, thinking becomes a source of distraction when we have a problem. This thinking being an idea, opinion, judgment, and comparison — which prevents us from looking, thereby understanding and resolving the problem.

Unfortunately, for most of us, thinking has become very important. We may ask, "How can I exist without thinking? How can I have a blank mind?" To have a blank mind is to be in a state of stupor and our instinctive reaction is to reject it because we believe that without knowledge we cannot operate in this world. But surely a very quiet mind, a mind that is not distracted by its own thinking, a mind that is open and does not get distracted by the experience, can look at the problem very directly and very simply. It is this capacity to look without any distraction at our problems, without letting our past interfere is the only solution. For that, there must be a quiet, tranquil mind. Meditation means putting the mind aside so that it no longer interferes with reality and see things as they are.

Why does the mind interfere at all?

Because the mind is a product of society. It is society's agent within us. It is not in our service. It is our mind but it is not in our service and has been conditioned by society. Society has implanted many things in it. It is our mind, but no longer functions as a servant to us; it functions as a servant to society.

Meditation means putting the mind aside and just witnessing it. The first step is to love yourself. This will help us tremendously. By loving ourselves as we are, not as per the requirement of society, we can destroy much of what society has implanted within us. Once we accept ourselves as we are, we will become free from society and its conditioning.

Chapter 6 Body and Energy

Body – a scientific perspective

According to modern medical science, the basic unit of the human body is the cell. The cells make up the tissue; tissues collectively form an organ; organs integrated form a system and a collection of different systems like: nervous, respiratory, circulatory, digestive, excretory, endocrine, and reproductive — constitute the human body.

Body – a yogic perspective

Indian philosophy of Vedanta visualizes the human body, 'Sharira' in Yogic terms, as a collective phenomenon of the gross body (Sthula sharira), subtle body (Sookshma or Linga sharira), and the causal body (Karana sharira). The life span of each of the bodies is different as the gross body is made of 'Pancha mahabhutas' (5 elements) and is less when compared to the other two bodies.

Gross Body

This is the physical body. It comprises of the 'annamaya kosha' and the 'pranamaya kosha'. The physical body needs food, drink, and air which is got from the 'annamaya kosha'. The air is got from the 'pranamaya kosha'. The gross body is the physical body made up of the 'Pancha mahabhutas' — consisting of Earth, Water, Fire, Air, and Akash. The land is bones and flesh. Water is blood. Fire is body temperature (98.6° F). Air is respiration. Akash is the life force and life energy.

Our body and the earth are structured in a similar pattern. The bones are in the center, the flesh is stuck to bones, next is the blood and this is body temperature. Then comes the air circulation and finally the 'Akash' particles. Our earth has a heavy metal at the center. Metals like mercury are at the next level. The minerals like magnesium which are lighter than other metals are at the next level. Water circulation is above it and then comes absolute space.

Akash is the subtlest of all and Akash particles are present in the other four elements — Earth, Water, Fire, and Air. The Akash particles that fill the Universe are called 'mahakash'. When they come together and form air, fire, water, and solids, they are called 'bhoothakash'.

The Akash particles in living things is called lifeforce. Humans live only because of the life force. They are called 'chittakash'. This energy circulates along a well-defined path within the body and is referred to as life energy circulation. Life energy particles are so minute that we cannot use scientific measurement devices to measure this. But through meditation, sages were able to go deep into the bodies and perceive them.

Lifeforce particles are minute dust particles broken from absolute space. When they rotate speedily around the body, they release energy due to the compressive force of gravity. This dust particle that comes out of the life force particles is called magnetism. The dust particles that come out of the Akash particles in living things are called 'biomagnetism' and the dust particles coming out of the Akash in outer space are called 'universal magnetism'.

Subtle Body

The subtle or astral body (Linga Sharira) is a subtler sheath compared to the physical body and is composed of vital energy. This is the part of 'Pranamaya kosha', 'Manomaya kosha' and 'Gyanamaya kosha'. The prana or energy moves through the 'nadis' or channel and is controlled by the six chakras. The subtle body is responsible for our physiological functions namely: breathing, digesting, metabolizing, circulation, endocrinal, neural, skeletal, muscular, etc. Manomaya kosha is composed of two qualities, mana (mind) and buddhi (intellect). 'Gyanamaya kosha' is the sheath of the intellect (buddhi) and intuitive knowledge/wisdom.

The body follows the mind and every thought in the mind creates a vibration in our Linga sharira. This, in turn, gets transmitted to the physical body. In the physical body, it causes activity in the nervous matter of the brain. This activity in the brain causes electrical and chemical changes in the body.

Causal body or Karana Sharira

'Anandmaya kosha' resides in the causal body (Karana Sharira). The causal body needs bliss which it gets from 'anandmaya kosha'. The causal body is the doorway to the higher consciousness. It is associated with the state of dreamless sleep and samadhi. It links individual consciousness with collective consciousness. Experiences (samskaras) from our past lives are stored in the causal body. It carries the information and knowledge acquired during the previous births. The attachment of 'Maya' and intense desires for worldly objects and pleasures called 'vasanas' also go along with Karana Sharira.

Life energy center

The life energy which circulates within our physical bodies comes into existence when the ovum in the female is fertilized by the sperm of the male. Life energy circulation commences from the moment fertilization takes place and continues through every stage of growth and development of the fetus, till the death of the individual.

Universal magnetism and biomagnetism

When we look at the sky, we find a lot of stars. Beyond the universe, it is filled with endless space. We imagine the space to be a vacuum. But absolute space is not nothingness; it is the latent potential of everything in this universe. Space is called by other names like Brahman.

Lifeforce, as explained earlier, is the fundamental tiny energy particle. This energy particle has a whirling motion by which all masses are manifested. The energy particle is a fraction of the absolute space or static state and functions on an infinitesimal scale. Even though this energy particle is really a wave with a whirling motion, we assume it to be a particle because it reflects and refracts all the characteristic waves of pressure, sound, light, taste, smell, and mind.

This energy particle is the medium between the physical universe and the unseen subjective phenomenon, space. This energy particle starts revolving due to the compressive force inherent in the space (gravity). Due to friction of this revolving energy particle with static space, a dust particle-wave starts, this spreads continuously. This tiny unit of magnetic dust formed from the life energy cannot withstand the self-compressive force of space (gravity) and get transformed into a magnetic wave. This dynamic dust force or magnetic wave penetrates absolute space all around. The joint manifestation of dynamic force and static force (gravity or self-compressive) evolves as magnetism. So, the entire space is filled with formative dust, each of which is a tiny unit of magnetism. They produce magnetic waves due to spinning and travel all over the Universe. These magnetic waves are called Universal Magnetism.

Biomagnetism

Billions of life energy particles keep whirling all over the body. In each life-energy particle, millions and millions of formative dust particles function, energizing the life energy particle. The self-rotating and whirling life energy particles churn out the formative dust particles in the form of bio-magnetic waves. Thus, the churned-out formative dust particles form a field — a 'Biomagnetic' field, which is the basic force for the functioning of the body. Formative dust particles are magnetic. They are self-rotating and spread all over the body as biomagnetic waves.

This biomagnetism in the living things functions as the mind. This biomagnetism functions through our five senses. The cognition of these five input signals happens through the brain by the mind.

Five Tanmatras and Senses

The five elements or 'Pancha mahabhutas' manifest in the functioning of the five senses as well as in certain functions of human physiology. 'Tan' means subtle and 'matra' means elements.

The 'tanmatras'— the subtle elements are the objects of the five senses. The five 'tanmatras' are sound, touch, form, taste, and odor or smell. The five senses are hearing, tactile perception, vision, taste, and smell. The 'tanmatras' are the ways by which the objective world is sensed by the mind. We see light through our eyes, hear sound through our ears, smell through our noses, taste through our tongues, and feel the touch through the pressure on the skin. The magnetic waves transform five 'tanmatras' of pressure, taste, smell, light, and sound.

Let us take the example of a flower, the energy particles in the flower are in the constant rotation due to compressive force and because of this dust particles come out of these spinning particles as a repulsive force. This merges with the space outside and releases the energy of smell, or color based on the environment and finally dissolves into space. Our body has five senses. They have a perception, when the consciousness located at the core of the energy particle, cognizes the transformation of the biomagnetism that goes on in that sensory organ. In this case, the nose and eyes, on account of its clash with the waves emanating from the flower. The mind perceives the changes in the biomagnetism using the sense organs into the 'tanmatras' and transfers them to the genetic center with the assistance of the brain cells. So, our senses, the skin, tongue, nose, eyes, and ears cognize the transformation of magnetism into pressure, taste, smell, light, and sound respectively. Hence, the perception of the flower happens as — Cognition, Experience, and Discrimination.

Cognition: The magnetic waves emanating from the flower come into contact with biomagnetism from our senses (eyes & nose). The biomagnetism coming out of the eyes in form of light energy strikes the flower and comes to halt. It is unable to travel further and biomagnetism undergoes changes in accordance with the quality of the flower. When it returns through reflection, it is sensed by the consciousness in the body. This is cognition.

Experience: The magnetic waves coming from the flower mingle with the biomagnetism and travel to our genetic center (memory) where the consciousness incorporates it into the genetic center. This is nothing but experience. Experience is nothing but recognition based on our memory.

Discrimination: The consciousness in the genetic center (memory) compares the quality of the magnetic waves emanating from the flower with its past and perceives the difference between this and the one previously stored in it. This is discrimination, which is nothing but a process of classification of various experiences on the strength of the records already existing in the genetic center.

Relationship between body, life force, and mind

Life-force or energy cannot function without a physical body. This is the reason we should always respect our physical bodies. It is the basis of our existence in this world. The mind can function through the brain only if body and life energy exist.

For a healthy body, there should harmony between the body, mind, and life energy. If our body is not well, this will affect our mind. The health of our body is based on what we eat and how we exercise. This has an impact on the mind. This is visible when we do exercises or yoga. Hence, the body has a direct relationship with the mind.

The 'Pancha tanmatras' function with the mind in living beings. This is nothing but our six senses. In other words, when the biomagnetism circulating within the body, functions through the sense organs and the brain cells, it gives rise to the mind. When the biomagnetic waves emanating from the sense organs in a living thing come into contact with the energy waves emitted by objects outside, fluctuations occur, which is perceived by the mind. The mind is the product of the combined function of memory imprint, the brain cells (cognition), and the sense organs (input or perception). Mind is the final transformation of biomagnetism.

The relationship between consciousness and energy

Everything is energy; the only difference is the manifestation of it. Our body is energy; our mind is energy; our soul is energy. The difference is only that of different rhythms and different wavelengths. The body is gross energy functioning in a gross, visible way when compared to the mind which is less gross.

Mind is a little more subtle, but still not too subtle because we can close our eyes and see thoughts moving. They can be seen, if one is aware. They are not as visible as our bodies. Our body is gross and visible to everybody else too. Our thoughts are not visible to others and nobody else can see our thoughts.

The third and ultimate layer inside us — is our consciousness. It is not even visible to us. It cannot be reduced to an object; it remains the subject.

If all three energies function in harmony, we are healthy and whole. If these energies don't function in harmony, we become ill and unhealthy. We are no longer whole. To be whole is to be holy. To be whole, means our body, our mind, our consciousness, and all dances in one rhythm, togetherness, and deep harmony. They are not in conflict at all but in cooperation. The moment our body, mind, and consciousness function together, we have become the trinity and in that experience is the divine.

Desire and Energy

Our mind is always moving into the future and this movement into the future is desire. The desire is not about the object as the object of the desire may be God or Women, so it does not make any difference. Desiring is the about verb, not the noun, it essentially means we are not here. We are not in the present and the present movement is the only door into existence or reality. The past and future are not real as they are simply the projection of our minds.So in reality desire is worldly not spiritual as it takes us outside not inside. So it does not matter if one desires wealth, prestige, power, or desire for God, nirvana, or enlightenment, it is just a trick of the mind so every desire is worldly because desire is the world.So it is not a question of changing the desire, it is the question of a mutation, alchemy from a desire to no-desire and that is the real revolution. But how to move as this move is also a movement of desire. So understanding that any movement of the mind is desire is intelligence and this intelligence will act on its own and there is no need for an effort from our side.

All the religons have always talked about not having desires or atleast control of desires. The reason the scriptures have taked about desire is because desire is associated with wastage of our life energy and hence religions have mentioned not having any desire as a virtue. So understanding desire is very important as it could be misiterpreted as it is humanly not possible to live without any desires as desires are nothing but energy in form of thought projected into future.

The whole world is nothing but energy and religions call it by different names like Sakthi which literally means energy. So we are all nothing but energy at a different level and if the energy flows outwards as thoughts it becomes desire and there is a depletion of energy and we become weak. We may achieve what we desire but our spirit or soul would be empty and we won't be a content person. even if we manage to attain the entire world we will still be an unhappy and empty person inside.At birth all of us arrive with energy and death is nothing but losing all our life energy. But when a person dies without losing his energy, he does not comes back.At the time of birth, we are full of energy and life is nothing but losing or spending that energy, it is like a pot with a hole in it and we slowly become empty.We can accumulate energy during sleep and that is the reason we feel fresh in the morning. That is the reason humans become irritated or tired if one has not got a good night's sleep.Desire is one of the ways of losing energy and the most condensed form of desire is seeking pleasure either in sex or through intoxicants.The energy which comes from food can be saved by proper exercise. Part of this energy is used by the body to maintain itself. Energy is used by the body for converting the food we eat into the blood and also for the process of our brain.And when we have energy then our mind starts thinking. When we think about our future which is nothing but desire we lose our energy and when we think about our past it is mostly regrets and guilt about what we have done. This way the energy becomes a burden to the mind, as our mind is always occupied with some thoughts, and the only way to get some relief from this thinking process is to release energy in form of sex.If we look at our life without any discrimination it would look absurd as we collect energy and we are not able to handle that energy and hence we end up throwing that energy. It is sheer madness but we have no option and that is the reason for our frustration and dissatisfaction as nothing seems in our control, it is just a mechanical process of the mind that has a pattern and it seems that the entire humanity is not able to break free from that pattern.This cannot be the way to lead our life, something is definitely wrong. It is utterly meaningless to accumulate energy and throw it out because we are not able to manage it. It is like building a house and demolishing it because we are not able to live in that house. Some religious people have realized this and hence they go on fasting to stop accumulating energy, by this way, there is no energy to throw but then without this life energy life becomes empty and futile.

when energy accumulates on a very large scale and does not get dissipated by sex, then that energy begins to ascend within us. It is like a dam and with more water in the dam, the level of water starts rising and this increases the pressure and the height of the water starts raising. Generally when the energy starts accumulating it creates certain pressure or heaviness in our mind and this results in an increase in the frequency of our thoughts, this causes turbulance in our mind as what was inside our innermost mind (sub-conscious) starts coming to the top and we are not able to handel that thoughts and the only way to bring some peace to our mind is to unburden our mind by indulging in sex. Not that sex is taboo or bad it is just that sex at the physical level is fine but once it moves to the mind it becomes perversion, as all the time we are thinking about it. Just like eating is not bad but thinking about it all the time is not a good way of living.we are living at the first layer of our individuality which is the physical layer consisting of sex, here we can find joy only for a few minutes but if we allow the energy to accumulate then it will move upwards and open our second center which is the heart. Here the level of happiness changes, at the Physical level we need another person to make us happy but at the second center we alone are sufficient we can just be happy on our own as our life energy has become exuberant and we can feel the joy inside us. we no longer are afraid of being alone. Slowly when the energy accumulates and reaches the seventh center which is Sahasrar or the crown chakra, it is called Kundalini Energy, as our life energy has become one with the universal energy. Here the energy is at its peak as it has reached the destination, one becomes enlightened when this happens.

So does it mean we should do what priests have been doing for centuries, which is suppressing sex? If we suppress it or try to stop it we can never succeed as energy can never be stopped it will react just as strongly as the suppression. So Energy cannot be suppressed but it can be directed to higher centers, there are only two options either we give energy a new direction or release it which is nothing but wasting it.No one has become enlightened by suppressing sex, they have become enlightened only by activating higher centers, and by activating higher centers we become free of sex.Being celibate does not mean fighting with sex, it is just activating centers higher than sex. The church has been against sex and for thousands of years, saints have been suppressing it, and the more we block that energy more it pushes them and hence all their attention has been only at sex center and they could think nothing but sex. Their whole personality had become genital.

Energy and activation of other higher center

We need energy and we also need a system to give this energy a proper direction. So what are the requirements by which we can make this energy move upwards? They are
1. Staying in Present
2. Being Creative
3. Meditation

When one wants the energy to flow inside, towards the truth and godliness should reduce his wishes and desires in the future. Desire does not mean planning the work we have. There is a difference between planning and desiring the main difference is that in planning we deal with facts whereas in desire we fantasize about becoming something that we are not, here the object of desire is ourselves not facts.We should live here and now. When we are eating food, we should only focus on eating not on watching television or any other devices. whatever we are doing we should be doing it in totality with full awareness. It may sound or appear difficult but once we start doing it it will become easier.An emperor went to meet a zen mystic and a mystic was bringing water from the river, the emperor asked the mistic to share some wisdom and the mystic said "Sit and watch and learn". The emperor sat down and the mystic continued to bring water from the river. The emperor was confused and said, "would you say something too, all you are doing is bringing water from the river. The mystic replied " Watch carefully I am not here at all, only the action of bringing the water is happening. I do not exist at all, there is only the action there is no actor. It is only correct to say that I have become the action of bringing the water. Whatever we are doing we should do it with awareness and joy, not halfhearted.If we want to accumulate energy then we have to learn to live in present. There is great magic in the present. The present is self-contained like a pond. Any action that is done with totality is called virtue. Because completeness is called as poornam in Sanskrit and there is no duality when you are full hence there is no time or space and hence there is only our presence, not our personality.

The second requirement is to be creative because the energy of an uncreative person will want to flow through sex continuously. When a person is doing a mechanical job, his mind becomes heavy as there is no creative outlet for that energy. There is no outlet as there is no interaction with the outside world or nature. That is a reason soldiers who are doing repeated tasks daily feel the pressure to have sex. If our work does not allow creativity then we need to do something like singing a song, a person who loves singing will attain everything during singing itself and won't mind even if he is not praised. There should be some creativity and taking things not too seriously. Children are so light and the whole reason is that their lives are not serious it is just a game and their life is a play. A child playing is not serious and once he becomes serious, sex begins to enter his world. If we can jump or dance for an hour in the house we will find that heavy energy has been removed from our consciousness and it has become creative, it starts to flow upwards.

The third requirement is whenever you get a chance try to move inwards, we don't have to remain outwards for twenty-four hours a day because energy flows in the direction of what we are doing and if we do outwards that energy will flow outwards. Of course, this is better than doing boring mechanical work as our minds will become heavy by this energy and sex is the only way of releasing that energy. but when we do something externally continuously then we start losing our energy and this way we won't have any energy to move to the next center. inwards means sitting silently doing nothing. this is nothing but a form of mediation. that is the reason meditation helps in the evolution of humanity especially when one does it simply without any goals. as that would again mean a desire.

Chapter 7 Emotions

All our emotions have one thing in common — they are energies that overwhelm us and we are not able to stop or control the energy using our will. It can be any emotion: Anger, Love, Lust, or Hate. This overwhelmingness has no value by itself. It just shows that we are emotional. Any act born out of this overwhelm will be always wrong. Reduced to its basics, emotions make us lose our reasoning capabilities and our sensitivity. Love is not an emotion but an expression of our being. Emotions are not harmful unless we get identified with them. The identification can happen only through the mind. The source of all these emotions is our genetic center (memory). This has been true since the beginning of the human race. Man is violent and aggressive because he carries in him the animal traits and only through awareness and meditation can one be free from it. It cannot be overcome through suppression or cultivating virtue.

Emotion is very fragile and keeps changing. In one moment, it seems that it is all there is and at another moment, we are simply empty. So, if we want to create a stable platform, we need to cultivate some qualities. Initially, it will need awareness to cultivate them and later those qualities will become part of our being.

Harmonizing emotions

Any of the negative emotions like hate; anger can be transformed by bringing in balance. For example, if our mind is angry we have to bring in compassion by thinking about it and, immediately, the energy changes because they are the same because the opposite is the same energy only the name and form of that is different and the name is given by our mind. Once we bring compassion in, it absorbs Anger. We can try experimenting with it by keeping a statue of Buddha because that statue is a gesture of compassion. Whenever we are angry, we can go into the room, look at Buddha, sit Buddha-like, and feel compassion. Suddenly we will see a transformation happening within us: the anger is changing, excitement has gone. compassion arising. And it is not different energy; it is the same energy – the same energy of anger – changing its quality, going higher. This is not suppression of emotion Patanjali says ponder on the opposite: if we are feeling discontented, contemplate on contentment: What is contentment? And this will bring in the balance. This is the sublimation of emotion, not suppression. If we are angry and we suppress anger without thinking of compassion then it is suppression. Here the energy that was part of the anger still exists and we are just covering it with a smile and we act as if we are not angry – and anger is bubbling there and boiling there and ready to explode and this is suppression. In the case of sublimation, we are not suppressing anything, and we are not creating a smile or anything; we are just changing the inner polarity. The whole energy of anger becomes compassion – nothing is left to suppress. In fact, we have expressed it in compassion. Sublimation is using the energy in a higher way, the same energy being used with a different quality to it. But must apply it and then we will know how effective it is.

If we suppress our emotions, we can become so-called human beings -- bogus, superficial, hollow within; just dummies, not authentic, not real. And if we indulgence in emotion, we will become like an animal which is not bad, probably more beautiful than so-called civilized man, but just animals -- not alert, not aware, and not conscious of the possibility of the immense growth of the human potential. When we transform the energy there is a possibility of becoming divine which is the potential of all humans.

For true transformation or revolution, we need to inculcate four basic qualities. We had all of this when we were a child but it got lost later due to our need for security. The reason a Buddha is more alive than any other person is because of these four qualities: Friendliness, Compassion, Cheerfulness, and Gratitude.

Friendliness

Most of us get influenced by other people's opinions. If someone criticizes us, we become angry. When we are angry, we have more energy and this energy makes us feel more powerful and alive, but this energy is destructive.

Friendliness also has energy but it comes only when we take responsibility for our actions. When we blame others for all our misery, we automatically become hostile and angry.

Hitler wrote in his autobiography — "If you want to make a nation powerful, then pretend that you have enemies or create real enemies. Tell the nation that there are enemies everywhere and we will have to protect ourselves from them." All of Germany's strength came out of hostility; all of Japan's strength came out of hostility.

Historically, in the evolution of human beings, there was always a threat from the environment in the form of animals or enemies from another tribe. The threat brought a great deal of energy. But this energy is due to hostility and is directed to somebody outside us. If there were no one outside, hostility would not arise in us. When people believe that they are surrounded by enemies, it generates much strength and energy. This is the reason politicians or religious leaders need enemies. It makes others feel threatened, and using this fear, a religious leader can make people feel insecure and make them followers. These people will be emotional. They can be made to relate to any political or religious cause and be exploited.

But life is inside us and love is intrinsic. Friendliness is intrinsic. Hatred is triggered by the outside; love wells up inside. The emotions that are triggered by the outside are not love, although we may call it love. It is an attachment that makes love become hate in a relationship. This happens when others don't listen to us or act in a way that we like or want. What comes from outside is a reaction, an echo.

As soon as a child is born, he experiences fear and that is where the source of hatred is activated. The energy source of love is not activated. The friendliness within is only developed when one understands that the basic need for survival is present as an instinct and this makes him selfish and does not allow him to develop harmony with others. So, in the beginning, friendliness can start as a habit and once we act friendly, it activates the love within us, as people also respond to our friendliness. But here we need to do it with awareness and not in a mechanical way or for courtesy's sake.

This is the reason, in eastern culture, younger people seek the blessing of elders. This creates an environment of love and friendliness. Friendliness can begin from nature and later evolve to people, as it is easier to be friendly with a dog than with people. What we call friendliness in the west, is only hypocrisy and politeness. The friendliness is only an arrangement to escape from hatred, to avoid it. It is definitely not friendliness, although from the outside it appears to be.

Friendliness is a completely different thing. It can happen only if we are not ambitious. This is because ambitious people are in hurry to achieve success and are always worried whether they will attain it not. All their energy is focused on themselves. They are more interested in using people based on their strengths and weaknesses and consider them utility rather than as human beings.

All the powerful or successful people never have genuine friends as they have never genuinely invested in other people's well-being. Not that being ambitious is bad but the price for it is always loneliness as being ambitious means it is all about me and I use others as a tool to serve my purpose. And to overcome their loneliness they will be seeking.

This friendliness can also be initially activated through yoga meditating on the 'Anahata chakra' or heart chakra. Another way, is to do service or voluntary work that involves interacting and serving people without expecting anything in return.

The reason Buddha or Krishna could attract people was not because of their intellect but because of love. When a teacher or guru loves right, love becomes active inside thousands of people.

When a man is angry, he is angry at heart. Anger represents his helplessness and his ego's inability to accept reality. There is a heart in every person, even in the worst person. If we can touch it even once, the same person becomes friendly as a child.

A person who brings hate in others becomes full of hate and the person who brings compassion in others reaches the heights of happiness. The quality or perfume of a person is not external, it comes from the inside. Love is not an act born out of emotion or thought but from our life. Life inside us acts with love when we drop our self-centredness.

That is why we need to develop the source of friendliness. It needs to be developed in spite of all the primitive instinct for survival which has its source from animals. Mother Nature is only interested in our survival. Anything more than that has to be done on our own, it doesn't come naturally. So, love is something that needs to be awakened by us and it can be awakened by dropping our self or ego.

Compassion

Compassion is something deeper than friendliness. Friendliness is mostly a behavior that is cultivated by the culture and the environment where one is born. We are told to be polite to elders and give them respect from childhood.

Basically, friendliness remains as behavior in many people based on conditioning. It is something from me to the external world. It is one-way communication. There is no understanding of the other person. So, it is an artificial behavior from our side without understanding the other.

Compassion is something deeper than friendliness. People generally move from friendliness to compassion when they learn to ignore their Personal self or ego. Once we ignore our ego, which is nothing but an exaggerated sense of self-importance to our 'feelings', we give complete attention to others.

Once we look at others without any of our past emotions like hurt or anger, we will truly understand them and their behavior. Unless we truly understand that, we cannot develop true compassion for others. We will be too busy reacting to our sense of injured feelings and all our actions will be either to defend ourselves or criticize others.

Many times, it appears that even when we are friendly towards others, they are rude to us. Then, we start avoiding them. But if we don't become emotional and look at them without any judgment, we will find that their behavior towards us was not because of us but because they were in a state of mind in which we were not fully aware. Unless we realize their state of mind, we can never truly understand their behavior. Understanding their behavior requires no effort or skill but pure observation with a curiosity to know the reality instead of trying to do an analysis on their state of mind.

This is the reason we can understand the actions of our parents when we ourselves become parents. We have understood their state of mind as we ourselves are in that state of mind.

Compassion is like the light of a lamp. Even if there is no reciprocation from the other side, it will still continue to give out light. Whereas in attachment, someone can trigger our emotions. That is why there is no tension in compassion; it is a state of absolute calmness.

The emotions which have a source within and don't pull you from outside are emotions like compassion and love. Emotions that are created from the external environment from the people outside will always cause restlessness and become a source of worry and guilt.

The feelings which are intrinsic cause a sense of deep contentment and bliss. The response is from freedom as it is coming from within our being. It is not dependent on the other person. The other person may insult you, but you will not become angry.

Cheerfulness

As a child, all of us were cheerful but as we grew older, we become less and less cheerful. The reason is expectation. When we were a child, even small things would make us cheerful. The reason was our simplicity.

Simple people are always cheerful while those with a lot of expectations are never cheerful as they have left their happiness in others hands. It is not wrong or bad to have expectations and hope that things will occur as we expect them to. But when we depend on any external environment to make us cheerful, then being cheerful is not in our control and our happiness becomes dependent on others.

People like Socrates have faced death — laughing and happy. But a little unexpected rain, or a bus coming late, or a small mistake in a relationship like forgetfulness, can make us sit with long faces. This is about giving too much importance to our own idea of how things should happen.

It will always lead to misery and suffering as things may not always happen the way we want them to happen.

This should not be confused with the planning of events or things that are work-related. Those are acts that must be planned and worked upon like: building a plane, or a house, or an architect working on a building. But things that belong to the physiological realm like our desires may or may not come true. Our desires are of no existential reality, it is just a projection of our mind — usually a wish or a fantasy.

Our beliefs and opinions about ourselves are just our petty conclusions. They may be relevant to our ego but life in us is more important than ego. Life can happen inside us only we don't sustain our physiological dramas. For our life to be meaningful and joyful, cheerfulness is needed, and even more so in the case of a spiritual journey for which we need a spirit full of energy. If somebody compliments our son, saying that he plays football beautifully and if our mind has other images of him which are not so pleasant, then those images from the past will color the present. We can never become cheerful, as the past will act as a burden. Cheerfulness has nothing to do with the act or the work we are performing. We may not be happy with our salary but that emotion should not be allowed to spill over the action. The relevant work or the action should always be performed by us. Whether we complain about it and become miserable, or do the work cheerfully is entirely in our hands. Life may put us in a good situation or not so good situation, but we need to do the act or work. The question is whether do it cheerfully or grumble. If we allow external situations to influence us, we can never be free individuals. How we react should be in our hands and no external situation should dictate our reaction to that situation.

Being cheerful has nothing to with positive thinking. It has nothing to do with intellect and has to do only with emotion. Positive thinking is assuming that things will happen the way we wish them to happen. This is just our wishful thinking; there is no reality in it. Cheerfulness is not an outcome of positive thinking, which is nothing but self-deception. Cheerfulness is the emotion that we decide to have whatever the outcome, good or bad.

Life has to be transformed into joy. Even when life situations appear dark, it has to be made a joy. A person who succeeds in doing this is blessed and filled with joy.

Gratitude

Gratitude is something that is not of the mind and can never be acquired through behavior or effort. Gratitude comes to a person who has come out of his narrow set of opinions and conclusions, and his exaggerated sense of self-importance. It can happen only to those who are ready to surrender, who look at life as something more than just themselves and are not obsessed by their sensations, their security, and comfort.

Suppose we were dying of hunger and somebody gives us a piece of bread, tears of gratitude will come to us. If they had given us the same piece of bread at any other moment, or even if they had given us an entire loaf, it wouldn't have meant anything to us. But in that moment of hunger, you would look at the person giving you the piece of bread with enormous gratitude because you are overwhelmed by the selfless act of that person. Gratitude need not necessarily find expression in the form of eloquence; it could just be a look, a touch, or a blessing.

The whole process of yoga is to make us receptive to life in a deeper way — the ways that are not in our current experience of life. That is the only goal. Being overwhelmed with gratitude is a very beautiful way to be receptive. It can open people up in certain ways. The hardest part of working with people on the spiritual path is making them receptive. If they work on their own ability to receive, then giving them what is needed would be very simple. If one is hungry, it is not difficult to make him eat. But to make him hungry is a hard job.

The very process of life is a constant phenomenon of receiving. We have nothing of our own to give; receiving is all we can do. So, all one can do is receive gracefully and share. That is all there is.

Two days before death came to Rabindranath Tagore, he said, "Lord, how grateful I am! Oh God, how shall I express my gratitude? You gave this life to me when I was not in any way worthy of receiving it. You gave breathing to me when I had no right to breathe. You gave me the experience of beauty and bliss, which I had not earned at all. I am grateful. I am overwhelmed by your grace. This life of yours is very blissful and I am utterly grateful for it."

Gratitude is a straight path to freedom. We don't have to do yoga, meditate, search for gurus, discipline ourselves, or do anything else. Gratitude is an emotion filled with so much energy that it can transform stone into gold. This ultimate alchemy can happen only to very simple people, not those who are ambitious for money or power.

Ambitious people have the feeling of emptiness in them that needs to be filled by money, power, fame, or authority. But this emptiness can never be filled by those petty things they are after. They will always remain empty. Bhakti Yoga was a way in which many people got enlightenment simply by being filled with gratitude for life. But during the last century, achievement has been linked with success and it is almost impossible not to be influenced by society. Most of our needs are not actually ours. It is just something thrust on us by our society. Hence, it is very difficult to have gratitude in present times. In modern times, it is just about fulfilling our desires, our sensations, and our pleasure.

When gratitude happens, suddenly, we are happy for things in our possession, small or big. We see the same life with new eyes. If we had previously looked at life around us with our intellect or emotion, now a life filled with gratitude inside us is like looking at a life filled with love. It is just a perfect symphony.

Love and Hate

Love is a strange thing and as long as thought sustains it, it is only sensations, memories, images but definitely not love. Love cannot be a sensation, a pleasure. One cannot learn love. But if one removes hate, what remains is love. Hate is something natural in us. It is part of our instinct carried over from our past. Hate is something that needs to be attended to immediately because if there is no hate in us, there would be no exploitation, no wars, no division of rich and poor. There would be real harmony in this world.

But one cannot be taught how to love unlike teaching mathematics or science. What one can do is observe hate, as hate is something intrinsic in us. We cannot battle against hate or say hate is a bad emotion and try to suppress it. We have to just observe hate and let it drop as it is not important. What is important is not to let hate take root in our mind because our mind is like rich soil, and if given sufficient time, any problem can take root like a weed and become difficult to pull out. All problems initially are a part of our conscious mind and if we are not able to resolve them then and there, will get pushed to our subconscious mind. Later, it becomes a part of our memory or samskaras. Once it becomes a part of our samskaras, it will keep coming out in form of a thought.

Chapter 8 Meditation

After Buddha got enlightened, many questions were asked about God and truth. Buddha just smiled at the questions about God. He neither confirmed that there is God nor denied God. Finally, people asked him the difference between the state before he got enlightened and after his enlightenment. He just smiled and replied, "I am awake now".

When the mind is in a constant state of projecting things on the world or people around us, we are not in touch with life. We are just projecting our state of mind and hence are not awake.

People have different notions about meditation and how to do it, the main question is what is meditation. Meditation is not concerned with reason; it is irrational, not intellectual. Meditation is something that cannot be explained; it is something that happens. If someone tries to understand meditation then it would simply translate into sitting alone doing nothing, so there is no way that anyone can understand meditation. Meditation is not concerned with logic, reason, or vain arguments. We cannot analyze it at all. The only way to know it is to do it.

What can a restless mind know? What can it search for? It is so involved in itself that it cannot look in any other direction. Deep peace, total silence, and a totally relaxed state of mind are required for knowing the truth, and such a state of mind is required for meditation. In meditation, we don't have to go anywhere, the truth will come to us.

For meditation, a silent mind is a prerequisite. Although meditation cannot be taught and has to be done by individuals themselves, there are techniques to prepare the mind for meditation. It is like preparing the ground for the plants to flower, even though a flower blooms on its own. Preparing good soil is necessary for its blooming.

The chattering of the mind

Instead of asking how to make the mind silent, if we wonder why our mind keeps chattering and if we can understand the reason or cause for that, then that understanding will keep the mind silent on its own. It has understood or realized the reason for chattering.

The difference between understanding and realizing is that understanding is always at an intellectual level and hence the mind stores it as information or knowledge but the realization is something that will free the mind from that problem itself.

Realization can only happen on its own by the individual himself, it cannot be got through books or others. But intellectual understanding is the first step and as long as one understands that he has only the knowledge and has not got the realization, it won't lead to self-deception. Without this awareness, the ego will get strengthened by knowledge.

So, why do the human minds chatter, and why does the chattering bother us? There is a wastage of energy when our mind keeps on chattering but the reason it disturbs us is that our life can be peaceful only if our mind is silent. If the mind keeps on chattering, or if there is a constant disturbance, we lose our peace. The mind has to be in our control or else we lose our peace.

Peace is something that everyone should enjoy otherwise we will not be able to give our best in our professional and personal life. If a person does not have peace, he will not be able to concentrate or excel in his profession. The world needs people who are good at their work. The world needs good doctors, good engineers, good lawyers, and good teachers.

The origin of any thought can be only a memory. Without memory, there cannot be any thoughts. Our thoughts have their origin in our memory and there are different types of memories.

These are called imprints or karmic imprints. This imprint is stored in our unconscious mind and was propounded by Sigmund Freud. Jung went one step further and said that there is a collective subconscious, which is a Universal version of the unconscious mind consisting not only of our ancestral memory but also memory from all other human races. We can just call it Karmic imprints.

These imprints are present in our genetic center, which is in the center of our body or at the spine end or at the 'Muladhara chakra'. Life energy which revolves around the body picks up these imprints, takes it into the brain, and activates the neurons. These neurons send electrical signals based on the content of the imprints. Hence, a set of neurons are activated for a particular thought based on the memory imprints from the genetic center.

All the imprints from the evolution of humanity are stored there. All the desires that could not be fulfilled are stored as a seed waiting for the right opportunity to sprout. This is the reason all religions have preached truth, virtue, and morality because all our actions, good or bad, are stored in our genetic center and these imprints get passed on to our children.

Once we have this understanding, we take responsibility for all our behaviors. The reasons for our behaviors are not due to the factors from the external environment but our own past acts stored as karmic imprints in the genetic center. Once we realize this, we naturally go inward as the source of how we act or react to any outward situation inside us and so the solution to this is also inside us. This understanding leads us to meditation.

Meditation

Meditation is the process of emptying the contents of our mind, which is nothing but our consciousness. Although meditation is something that happens on its own, there are techniques needed to remove the obstacles of the mind.

Meditation is nothing but being alert or aware of the present moment. Neither being alert nor being aware needs any technique, but thoughts are obstacles to being alert or being aware. There are some compulsive behaviors or mechanical patterns of our mind that do not allow us to be alert or aware. This behavior can be changed by techniques. Similarly, some techniques can remove emotions like guilt and anger. All these techniques prepare the ground for meditation but these techniques by themselves are not meditations.

Vipassana is one such technique where one just witnesses his thoughts. The entire vipassana or Buddhist meditation technique is based on creating awareness. Watching the breath is one of the easiest things, as breath is what is natural to our body. We don't need to take efforts to breathe and when we start observing our breath slowly, we can become aware of its movement, going in and going out. Our thoughts interrupt our observation and we realize this only after some time. Once we are aware that we are not observing our breath, we need to move our focus back to observing the breath.

All our thoughts remain thoughts, as long as we are aware of them. If we are not aware of our thoughts, it will become the thinker or in other words, the mind will take the shape of its thought. The tendency of that thinker would be based on the content of memory or karmic imprints.If the imprint is pleasure, then based on the quality and content, the thinker or the 'ego' will seek pleasure through the same behavior from which it had previously obtained pleasure — from the original imprint.

The original imprint is carried to the brain by the life energy. This imprint will activate the neurons, and thoughts will arise. Based on the quality of thought called 'vasanas' in Sanskrit, an entity (ego) will be created and that will seek the same pleasure. Once the mind experiences this pleasure, it will further strengthen the imprint at the genetic center and those thoughts will keep on arising. This is how habits are formed. Once this habit becomes regular, it becomes part of the behavior of the mind. If this behavior is sustained over a long period, it will become part of the emotion. This is the reason people who are addicted to alcohol and other substances get emotional when they don't get their pleasure.

Being aware of the entire process of how our mind works is self-knowledge. This alone can free us from the tendencies of our minds. Self-knowledge leads to awareness. Awareness leads to meditation.

Shiva — The Destroyer and the Dancer

Shiva is a God in the Hindu religion associated with destruction. He is known as the destroyer. To destroy, we need energy and Shiva's wife is Sakthi, which means energy in Sanskrit.

He is known to shut his eyes and go into deep meditation for years. Shiva is a meta-physical representation of 'shoonya' or total emptiness of the vast universe. It is the highest form of energy that is in seed or static form. When the energy takes the form of motion, creation starts and is represented by the cosmic dance of Shiva. Shiva as a dancer represents the universe, which is the macrocosm. Shiva as a meditator represents the microcosm, which is nothing but the life energy inside all humans.

The energy representing Shiva which created the entire universe is also inside us as our life energy. This life energy is just pure energy. It cannot be labeled as good or bad. Shiva is not known for his etiquette or nice behavior. He is not good or bad, he is just intense.

This energy is ours and being the most evolved species in the universe, it is our freedom to do what we want with this energy. This energy can create anything that we wish to use in our minds. Hence, this energy creates our world based on our thoughts from our karmic imprints. So, if we just free up this energy from the projection of our mind based on our karmic memory, Shiva will start his cosmic dance inside us. This is something that can be experienced not explained. There is perfect harmony between the internal world (Microcosm) and the external world (Macrocosm).

Energy and Transformation

All movement and action represent energy. If we can make it intense, we can perform incredible things or the energy can be lost in the form of anger and hate.

Whenever the source of intense energy is tremendous desire or ambition, the energy is channelized into individual fulfillment, which gives the individual a sense of achievement and pride. But there is no transformation of the individual's consciousness representing his mind. He is still the same petty individual, repetitive, habitual, self-centered, without any real transformation, except he is traveling in an expensive car and living in an expensive house.

The energy at the Source is pure and intense but it gets dissipated due to different fragments in our minds. The energy passing through our fragmented mind gets dissipated, just like a pure light gets fragmented by passing through a prism. So, the only question is when does this fragment cease to be a fragment. One of the fragments could be to become famous and successful, another could be to become peaceful. Likewise, there are many fragments. These fragments have been created mostly by the conditioning of society and by the individual's likes and dislikes.

When the individual lets go of his individual self, then the energy dissipated through that 'becoming' is stopped. Then, this energy that is moving has no center to limit itself and hence becomes an unlimited space without the center 'I'. Now, the energy, which is Sakthi, will become Siva, as there is no movement. Shiva can now take the form of the destroyer, and there is a mutation of the karmic imprints at the cellular level. When there is silence in the mind, or when the mind falls silent, the energy is at its height.

Whenever, there is any movement of the mind through desire or ambition, either into the past or present, it is a process of 'becoming'. The brain cells or neurons get activated and energy takes that form projected by the mind. When the mind is free from any thoughts or movement and is silent, the energy is completely dormant but highly intense, and this intense energy transforms the mind. The point is not how to awaken or obtain this energy but realizing that any movement the mind makes will lead to the dissipation of this energy, and then it will not transform our individual consciousness.

Ordinarily, the energy is moving away from us towards things and targets in the world. The energy is moving away from us and we feel drained. The energy goes away and never comes back. We go on throwing away energy. By and by we feel dissipated and frustrated. Nothing comes back and we start to feel empty. The Life energy is just oozing out every day and finally comes death.

The greatest miracle in life is to understand this and turn the Life energy towards the inside, towards home. It is a turning-in. It is not that we leave the world. We live in the world. There is no need to leave anything or go anywhere else. We live in the world but in a totally different way. Now we live in the world but we remain centered in ourselves. Our energy goes on returning to ourselves. We are no longer out-going; we have become in-going. Of course, we become a pool of energy, a reservoir, and energy is a sheer delight; energy that is overflowing. We are in delight and we can share and give in love.

Wherever we go, whatsoever we do, we always do in the inner light — with awareness. That is what meditation is all about — to become more alert. Live the same life, just change our alertness —make it more intense. Eat the same food, walk the same path, live in the same house, be with the same woman, with the children, but be totally different from your inside. Be alert! Walk the same path but with awareness. If we become aware, suddenly the path is no more the same, because we are no more the same. If we are aware, the same food is not the same because we are not the same, the same woman is not the same because we are not the same. Everything changes with our inner change.

Agnya meditation [Third eye of Shiva]

Once we realize that we are prisoners of our mind and that any movement of our mind will only strengthen its movement and only in silence there can be mutation, then the mind will automatically become silent. This is because we have seen the truth of it. We will be out of the games of our cunning minds.

Just realization that any movement will make us a prisoner of our mind will free us from prison. The first step is the last step. There are no steps between the first and the last step. Once we are free from our thoughts which are nothing but free from all the conditioning stored in our memory, all the karmic imprints in our subconscious mind (genetic center) will come out. This is nothing but the sum total of entire humanity.

All the violence and sex will come out. Once we are aware of those thoughts in our mind, just pure awareness with all our attention, without fighting them or indulging them, just witnessing them without any movement, then the life energy will burn those imprints. Pure energy will interact with those patterns and make them dormant. Karmic seeds will get burned by the energy and these imprints or samskaras won't be able to sprout again. At the core of all humans are our karmic imprints. The core is not something beautiful or good. The core is just an instinct that seeks security and pleasure.

Meditation implies no movement in form of thought — that is a silent mind. Meditation in daily life is the transformation of the mind, a psychological revolution. It is required so that we can live daily life in pure energy with compassion, love, and vitality to transcend all the pettiness, the narrowness, and the shallowness of the human mind.

Meditation and Love

Meditation means being ecstatic in our aloneness. But when we become ecstatic in our aloneness, soon the ecstasy is so much that we are not able to contain it and It starts to overflow on us. And when it starts overflowing it becomes love. Meditation allows love to happen. And the people who have not known meditation can never know love. They may pretend that they love but they cannot. They will only pretend -- because they don't have anything to give, they are not overflowing.

Love is sharing. But before we can share we must have it and for that Meditation should be the first thing. Meditation is the center; love is the circumference of it. Meditation is the flame; love is the radiation of it. Meditation is the flower; love is the fragrance of it. When we start overflowing, we start relating with others, caring for others -- service comes into our life as a shadow of meditation. It is not to be imposed upon us like a duty. 'Duty' is a four-letter, dirty word. Whenever we do something AS a duty, it is imposed, cultivated, and phony. It is pseudo, it makes us a hypocrite.

Western society lives under an affliction because of their ignorance about meditation because whatever they do is out of their intellect. And the mind can never be the source of joy. It can only create agony, but never ecstasy. Mind is our hell. So we have to learn to become meditative and let our creativity be secondary to our meditativeness instead of our intellect.

Chapter 9 Awareness

Generally, all of us are aware of things around us. When we look at a sunrise, we are so absorbed in the beauty of the sunrise that we completely forget that there is a greater beauty that is making it possible for us to know the beauty of the sunrise — our awareness or consciousness. Currently, our awareness is focused on external objects — the sunset, the sunrise, the moon, the mountain, etc. If we just drop the object, what remains is pure awareness.

There is no other value that is higher than awareness. Awareness is the seed of godliness in humans. Awareness will lead us to the fulfillment of our destiny. As we go deeper and deeper into awareness, our actions may not be efficient but they have a new quality, the quality of grace, which is far more valuable. No machine can have the quality of grace. Our actions and words will have a beauty of their own.

Only awareness can free our minds. Once our ego is silent, not made silent by will or effort or discipline, then the other part of the mind which is 'Intelligence' can enter our life. The unknown can enter the known (memory). Here, the unknown is not known by our intellect (buddhi) or felt by the ego (mind) as it is not a part of memory (manas). Chit or intelligence is something live and filled with a subtle energy that our memory cannot capture. It enters our consciousness, transforms it, and all our actions will be based on pure awareness, not a reaction based on our experience.

Introspection and Awareness

Introspection is sometimes done by our mind, generally after a failure. So, it is an activity performed by our intellect (mind) using our stored-up memory (manas). Our memory is not all-inclusive and is limited by nature. Introspection is generally done to improve oneself or to change or to become something. If I am angry, I introspect to find out the cause of my anger. Introspection will always lead to depression as the entity which does the analysis is also the mind. The mind being a limited entity can never give any clarity or solution to any problem related to itself. Whereas awareness is something that happens when you observe the anger without any condemnation or judgment. So, when we are angry and we are aware of it, it is like being with a fact, and hence there is no need for will or effort. Will or effort is required only when we want to control the anger or try to move away from anger. When one is angry and is aware of it, there is no effort or discipline required; there is no question of effort required to be aware of anger. When one is aware of the anger, it will lead to the realization of the cause of anger and that frees the mind of anger. Choiceless awareness will lead to freedom.

Awareness and consciousness

A child is always spontaneous because he is not conditioned by the world on how to behave. He is genuine and spontaneous but his behavior comes from his subconscious. The spontaneity is there but the source is not the conscious mind, it comes from his instinct which is nothing but a part of his subconscious mind.

There are two types of people — first, those who are unconscious and innocent. They are childish and get hurt as they grow up and interact with society, as each society has a behavior pattern. Then, there are individuals who are conscious and have lost their spontaneous nature because of the discipline required to fit into the pattern of society.

They are conscious but have lost their spontaneity and hence lost the beauty of life. They were smart enough to realize the ways of the hypocritical society and hence their response is always guarded, not natural, and hence not spontaneous. When a person is aware and responds with spontaneity, the source of response is not from a past memory. The spontaneity is there and in the background of consciousness is awareness.

Awareness and Mind

When awareness increases the activities of the mind get diminished. The intellect of the individual thrives on comparison and measurement. A child has been conditioned from early stages to become an achiever. Naturally, his sense of self-esteem is based on how successful he is in this society. To become successful, a person has to become efficient. Efficiency comes with practice and repetition in a specialized field. This makes the mind mechanical as it has to repeat the act many times to perfect it. Awareness is the opposite of the mechanical mind. Society is conditioned for efficiency and hence society has created individuals who have become mechanical. This creates a robot-like behavior in every individual. They are without awareness of the surroundings or people around them.

This mechanical behavior is rewarded in society as it is considered more efficient. Hence, all educational and academic institutes reward those students who are quick and fast. A person who can solve problems quickly is considered more efficient than a person who takes more time to understand the problem and see the beauty of it. In this educational system, when a student graduates, he becomes very efficient but without much awareness.

Every individual has an image of himself based on the way society and people around him treat him. The mind identifies itself with this image and a personality is created in this process. Such an individual feels insulted if he is not treated as per his idea of self-image. Pride is injured as they do not know who they are really and have identified themselves with the image given by society and their self-worth depends on how people around them treat them.

Society respects people who are famous and rich and hence the ego of these people always tries to keep its self-image intact. But all it would require is to break this image and once the image is broken, the ego becomes aggressive and reacts with violence. This is the reason for all the violence one sees around the world. The ego is responsible for this. Awareness is something that can slowly open up the intelligence (chit) of our minds. A gap is created by this awareness and breaks the mechanical part of the mind. The gap allows the Chit, something which is not part of memory (manas) to enter. This is nothing but intelligence. Then, the person instead of reacting to the situation will slowly observe, take some time, and then respond. If the reply is from memory, it is still part of the old mind (Buddhi) and contradiction will persist. But if it is from the new part of the mind untouched by memory, then it will resolve the problem.

To remove this ego with awareness is very important for both — the individual and society. Here, the removal is not an act of the mind. Just like when the light comes, the darkness disappears, when there is awareness, there is no mind.

Any work done with passion and awareness will change the very quality of work. It is no longer just a physical act. It is no longer just a physical release; it is a very deep experience of life. It is a tremendous experience of no mind. It is a door towards the greatest spiritual possibility.

Three steps — consciousness, witnessing, awareness

Unconscious activity is the state of all our minds. There are hundreds of thoughts in our minds and we are not conscious of most of our thoughts or emotions. Through consciousness, we can achieve witnessing, and through witnessing we can achieve awareness. Through awareness, we can achieve 'no-mind'. After awareness there is nothing; awareness is the end. Awareness is the end of all spiritual progress. If we become one hundred percent conscious, we become a witness, a 'Sakshi'.

If we become a 'Sakshi', we have come to the jumping point from where the jump into awareness becomes possible. In awareness, we lose the witness, and only witnessing remains. We lose the doer, we lose the subjectivity, we lose the egocentric "me". There is no actor; there is only acting. There is no dancer; there is only dance.

Then, consciousness remains, without the ego. The circumference remains without the center. This circumference without the center is awareness.

Consciousness without any center, without any source, without any motivation is awareness.

So, we move from the unaware existence that is matter, 'Prakriti', towards awareness. We may call it the divine or godly, and the only difference between matter and the divine is the level of consciousness.

Awareness is the key

For any lock, we need a key to open it. For all problems caused by the mind, there is a simple key — awareness. One may wonder, how awareness can help when the mind seems to be uncontrollable and how awareness can function as key.

When a person is sleeping, he dreams that he is surrounded by enemies who are trying to kill him and he tries to run. But the enemies surround him. He shouts for help and suddenly he wakes up and realizes that it was nothing but a dream. There were no enemies and he needed no saving. But in the dream, he had tried every possible way to protect himself and was finding it impossible. This is the case with us and with everybody.

Buddha after being enlightened said, "This is unbelievable! I have been enlightened from the very beginning!? All those chains and all those imprisonments were just dreams !?" People would gather around Buddha and ask him questions like — "How can one be free from worry and anger? How can we stop ourselves from being obsessed with sex or food?" For all the questions, he would give awareness as the solution. His disciple, Ananda, listening to this asked him how he was prescribing the same answers to different kinds of questions. Buddha replied saying, "Their illnesses seem different just as people can dream different dreams. But the solution for all is just to be awake".

Awareness and freedom from pleasure

Why has man pursued pleasure through power, prestige, fame, and money for ages? Why is there a demand for pleasure through drinks, sex, music, or God? If we observe the facts of pleasure, man has pursued it for ages. It is one of the major factors of our consciousness. Pleasure is sought in various forms. Knowledge is a form of pleasure — the pleasure of reading many books and appearing intellectual. There are other pleasures to like: the pleasure of possession and the pleasure of detachment, the pleasure of austerity and the pleasure of abundance, the pleasure of achievement and the pleasure of renunciation and going around the village with a begging bowl wearing a loincloth. Why have we as human beings pursued pleasure and have given so much importance to pleasure? Is Joy a pleasure? Seeing a beautiful child or a beautiful flower, a peculiar sensation arises inside our body, and thought recognizes that as the state of joy and the mind wants more of it. Pleasure is a movement of thought. I had a good meal yesterday and I say to myself, I must have it again.

The pleasure is the movement of thought over an incident that happened in the past and which is stored up as memory. The movement of thought is a pleasure. There is delight or joy when we see a snow-capped mountain or a beautiful sky, or there is an appreciation of the vast world. Here again, thought moves over it to memory and makes it out to be a pleasure.

The brain stores all the information that it receives through the senses for safety and security reasons. The brain cannot function without security and hence it stores all information as knowledge so that the mind can use it again. However, because of this memory, the thought process always brings incidents, which it experiences as pleasurable and avoids those situations that it considers as unpleasant or not pleasurable. This repetition makes the mind mechanical or repetitive in nature.

There is a part of the brain which is mechanical and another part of the brain which has never been used by thought. Thought has not entered this part. We can find out about this part only if the registration process comes to a stop. So, the real question is — can the brain be fully aware of any situation and no recording takes place however pleasurable or painful that situation maybe? Because, if there is no recording of any incidents, then we will be free from the chains of the past.

If the mind can be fully aware, then there is no recording of the incident by the mind as the mind ceases to exist — in total awareness. There is no recording as intelligence is responding to the situation and intelligence is something beyond memory. If we just try it out in real life, we will know what it means to be fully aware.

Chapter 10 Freedom

Freedom is mostly associated with external things and physical surroundings that we find restrictive, like an autocratic government or a jail. The desire to act without any restriction is also seen as freedom, particularly in the western world. The outward expression of freedom is considered very vital there.

Many in the western world consider wealth as a source of security and hence consider economic freedom as something every individual should attain. Many consider possession of wealth and money as the route to economic freedom.

The freedom to do anything, which is freedom of expression, is also not real freedom because wanting or desiring to do something arises out of our minds. The mind is our bondage and is compulsive by nature.

The next is freedom from something, like an abusive partner in a relationship. But freedom from something is also not true freedom. It is not freedom because it is still something that is given to us; there is a cause to it. It is the opposite of that 'something'. The thing that we were feeling dependent on is still there in our freedom. We are still obliged to it as without it we would not have been free.

True freedom has nothing to do with external situations or the world. It is not political or economic. Political freedom can be always taken away by those who are more powerful than us. Economic freedom can just disappear like a dewdrop facing the sun. They can never be in our control. What is in our hands or something that cannot be taken away from us can only be considered as true freedom? True freedom is only spiritual freedom. It has to do with our innermost and cannot be chained or put into prison. Our soul is intrinsically free, we don't have to struggle for it, it is always available to all, we just need to turn inwards. Neither the past nor the future has an existential reality, they are just thought processes of our mind and freedom from thoughts means real freedom.

If we enquire deeply into what freedom means — we always react to the external environment based on our past experience or our karmic memory. Thus, real freedom should be from our tendencies based on our memory, which is nothing but our mind — the mind with its compulsive nature of seeking pleasure and avoiding pain.

So, how is one to be entirely free from those impressions? How do we gain such freedom?

Throughout history, we have been assured by leaders and scriptures that if we perform some rituals, repeat some prayers or mantras, suppress our desires, control our mind, sublimate our passions, limit our appetites and refrain from sexual indulgence, we shall, after sufficient discipline of the mind and body, realize freedom. This is what all the religious seekers and monks have done throughout the ages. They have cut themselves off from society, stayed in isolation in the desert, mountains or cave, or wandered from village to village with a mendicancy bowl. They discipline their minds to adapt to a pattern given by the religious authority.

But a tortured, broken mind, an arid mind that wants to escape from all turmoil, which has denied the outer world and that been made dull through discipline and conformity, however hard and sincerely it seeks, will find only illusion based on its own distortion. It will not find reality. It will always find a projection of what is present in its memory, nothing new can enter.

What can one do when one truly realizes that no book or knowledge can help us? This leads one to realize how one is conditioned by society. If we cut off every knowledge given to us by society, then one realizes that one knows absolutely nothing, one is just empty, and how heavily one is conditioned by society. Once we realize that we know nothing, we will become attentive to all the things around us. P. D. Ouspensky, a famous writer, had heard about George Gurdjieff, a Russian philosopher, mystic, and spiritual teacher, and wanted to learn from him. So, he met Gurdjieff and asked him to teach him. Gurdjieff gave him a blank paper and pencil and asked him to write down the things he already knew so that Gurdjieff won't have to teach him those things.

P. D. Ouspensky himself was a writer of many books, so he wrote down a list of things he thought he knew. He realized that Gurdjieff was a master and he will question those things and unless he had really understood that thing Gurdjieff won't let him go. So, he went through the list again and when he looked at each item, he realized that he had only bookish knowledge about those subjects but not actual realization. Slowly, he removed the items one by one, and suddenly, he realized that he knew nothing. All he knew was somebody's knowledge, not his own. He panicked and ran with an empty paper to Gurdjieff, threw the paper down, and shouted, "I don't know anything." Gurdjieff smiled and said, "Today's class is over. Come tomorrow for the second class."

So, being aware of "what one is" which is self-knowledge is the first step towards freedom. Freedom cannot start from a common point. It has to start from one's centre, which only that individual can be aware of. Freedom is not something that can be given by one to another. Freedom is something that everyone must discover for themselves.

Stages of freedom

When a child is born, it depends on parents for survival. As it grows, it is conditioned by society
and its inherent karmic imprints in the form of memory from its parents. What Nietzsche would call as 'camel phase' is where the child has to assimilate all the conditions and teachings by the books and religious leaders. Nothing wrong in reading about different religions as, without initial conditioning of what is right and what is wrong, the child may get lost completely at the early phase of life. It is needed for the security of the child. It is part of growing up — nothing wrong with it.

But there is something inside man that won't allow him to rest. He will always want more. He may not understand what he wants, so he will always expand the on things his mind knows — wealth, fame, and success. Through those, he hopes to achieve happiness.

The second phase is called the 'Lion phase'. He will become very ambitious and very active and once he achieves those things, he will realize that all his wealth and fame has not given him happiness. Here, he can either search for true freedom or just maintain his position and lead an increasingly mechanical life which will make his mind dull. He will try to forget himself by indulging in acts that will give him pleasure, which is the church, sex, or drinks.

In the first phase, the mind is dull and is 'Tamasic' in nature. It was just seeking security and survival. It is comparable to the larva stage of the caterpillar. There is no movement, dynamism, or energy. It is just static without any life. Many people grow and die in this stage. In the second phase, the Lion, the mind is 'Rajasic' in nature. Here it is comparable to the caterpillar stage where there is movement and a lot of energy but there is no peace or happiness. Many people, especially in the western world, belong to this stage. The people in this stage have money and comfort, but happiness and peace prove to be elusive.

The third phase is the 'butterfly phase'. The child stage was assimilation; the lion stage was being independent and trying to achieve peace. The third phase is the butterfly which indicates freedom from past or memory. The butterfly is not cocooned by its past in the form of memory and is independent of the past and becomes creative. Here the mind is of 'Sattvic' nature. The energy is highly intense and the mind is calm and peaceful by its nature without any need for stimulation from the external environment.

The first stage is given by society, the second stage has to be attained by the individual. For the third stage, you either need the grace of God or the guidance of a person who has already attained that stage. Even an extremely gifted person like Friedrich Nietzsche who had obtained a Ph.D. in his younger days and become a professor at a remarkably young age of 24, died due to mental illness at the age of 55.

Knowledge through a book will lead to only intellectual understanding but not clarity. Clarity comes only through realization. There are two types of learning — one is acquiring and accumulating a great deal of knowledge through experience and books. This type of knowledge is fine for making a living in this world. One will develop skills that are required in society and can be very successful in his profession. This will generally lead to self-importance and give the individual a sense of confidence. But this is confidence without any clarity of mind. So, when life throws them a problem or challenge, they will try to address the problem without understanding the real cause of it and later themselves become a problem.

Whereas a person with clarity of mind, a mind without any sense of exaggerated self-importance will look at the problem without any past memory influencing him. He will be able to understand it as — each time the problem is new and we cannot address it using the mind that is anchored in the past. Real understanding can happen only when the content of our consciousness, or what we call 'my mind' is empty of experience and knowledge — when it is silent. When the mind is empty, transformation happens at the energy level, not at the physiological level, which is an act of the mind. Transformation at the physiological level can never awaken the intelligence in us. The transformation that seems to happen due to the mind by following a strict discipline or adhering to a blueprint is just a form of self-deception and not real transformation.

Freedom means Insight or Clarity. One has understood the game of society and one remains without any clinging to society or relationships in the name of love or hate. The mind has no impact. Even though we may live in this world, we no longer belong to it. This is not being insensitive, but being aware of the true nature of society.

Three types of freedom

There are three types of freedom. These three types have to be understood well. The first is 'freedom from'. Here, we are a prisoner of something. The second is 'freedom for'. Here, we need the freedom to achieve something. The third is just freedom — neither from nor for. The first 'freedom from', is a reaction. It is past-oriented. We are fighting against the past. It is something we want to get rid of, like the memory of an abusive husband or a bad relationship in past. It is something we want to get rid of it because we are obsessed with it.

Psychiatrists try to give us this freedom. Freedom from past traumas, childhood wounds, and pains. Primal therapy is based basically on past traumatic experiences of early childhood. We have to go backward to free ourselves from the past. We have to reach the first primal scream and then we will be free. For primal therapy, psychoanalysis, and for other therapies, the memory from the past has to be dropped. We have to fight with it, we have to somehow disentangle ourselves from our past karmic imprints, and then we are free.

As far as this freedom is concerned, both Karl Marx and Sigmund Freud are not opposed to each other. Both Karl Marx and Sigmund Freud say that one has to become free from the past — all past social structures, economic structures. Karl Marx's approach is political. Sigmund Freud's approach is psychological. But both are rooted in the idea of freedom from the past.

All political reforms are reactions to a particular situation and are always fragmented. One fragment against another — us vs them. This has to be realized. It only gives us an appearance of freedom, but it is never true freedom. Out of a reaction that has its source in the past, total freedom is not possible. All political reforms are reactions is based on past patterns, only through action and not reaction is their real freedom. Action that is free from the past is nothing but our memory, our experience, our likes, and our dislikes.

We can go against the past, but just by being against it, we are caught and have got in through the back door. An entity that sees the past is a product of that past memory. That is why we become like whomsoever we are fighting with. We have to choose our enemies very carefully because we will be determined by them! For fighting with them, we will have to learn their strategies, we will have to learn their ways. Slowly, enemies become very alike — more alike than friends.

The second idea is 'freedom for'. It is future-oriented. The first is political; the second is more poetic, visionary, utopian. Many people have tried that too but is also not possible, because future-oriented people can't live in the present. We have to live in the present. Visionaries can only imagine but never implement. Beautiful utopias always have been imagined, but those utopias never become reality. They cannot become reality.

If we react to the past, we are determined by the past. If we forget the past and look at the future, we are still driven by the past, we are just not aware of it. Looking at the future, we dream beautiful dreams, but they can't change reality. The reality remains the same. Dreams are very ineffective and impotent. The reason for our dreams is that we are trying to escape from our present with which we are not happy. Dreams are nothing but a reaction of our minds to escape from the dull and insipid life one is leading.

'Freedom from' is a reaction. 'Freedom for' is revolution. The third — just freedom, is a rebellion. It is present-oriented. The first is political, the second is poetic, and the third is mystical and religious. What we mean by 'just freedom' is just being fully aware of the present moment. In observation, it is being free from the memory, just a choiceless awareness because choice means duality. Neither for nor against, no past, no future, just being here now, just living moment to moment with no ideology, with no utopia.

The real yogi, the real mystic, is not against the past and is not for the future. He is so utterly fully absorbed by the present that he has no time and no energy for the past and the future. This is how rebels are born. The rebel is the most beautiful phenomenon in the world. Buddha is a rebel, Jesus is a rebel, so is Krishna. They are rebels. We will misunderstand them if we think they were revolutionaries; they were not. Neither were they reactionaries. Their orientation is different; their orientation is here and now. They don't live for an ideal, and they don't live against any ideal. They don't have any ideas. No ideology exists in their consciousness.

They live in the sheer purity of this moment. They live it, enjoy it, sing it and dance it. When the next moment comes, they live the next moment with the same joy and the same cheerfulness. They move moment to moment. They don't plan. They are so enthralled in creator's creation that they don't have time to indulge in their own physiological drama created by their mind.

Two sides of freedom

Freedom has two sides. If we experience only one side of it, we will feel freedom mixed with a tinge of sadness. So, we have to understand the whole psychology of freedom.

The first side is freedom from nationality, from a certain church, from a certain race, from a certain political ideology. This is the first part of freedom, the foundation of freedom. It is always from something. Once we have attained this freedom, we will feel very light, very good, and very happy. For the first time, we will start rejoicing in our own individuality, because our individuality was covered with all those things that have been given to us by society and now, we have become free of it.

But this freedom is only one-half of it. With it comes sadness too, because the other half is missing. 'Freedom from' is fulfilled, but freedom for what? Freedom from something in itself is dangerous without a purpose because being free could mean one can choose any path. The structure that was holding him is no longer there and without taking responsibility for that freedom, the individual can become lethargic and go into the path of destruction. This can be observed in the soldiers who have come back from the army. They have freedom now but without a goal or a path, they just waste themselves as they don't have the discipline of the army that could hold them together.

There should be meaning. It is freedom for something, something creative — the freedom to sculpt, freedom to dance, freedom to create music, poetry, painting. Unless the freedom turns into a creative realization, we will feel sad because we will see that we are free, our chains are broken and we no longer have any handcuffs, we are free from the prison created by our mind, we are standing under the starry night, completely free, but we don't know where to go. This realization leads to sadness about what path to choose. Up to now, there was no question of going anywhere — we were imprisoned. Our whole consciousness was concentrating on how to get free. Our only anxiety was how to get free, and once we are free, a new kind of problem will arise — what to do now that we are free?

Just freedom in itself does not mean anything unless we choose a creative path. We can either go deeper into meditation for self-realization or if we have a certain kind of talent that has not been allowed to develop because of our fear, we could do that now as our hands are no longer in chains. Then, our freedom is complete, the circle is complete.

'Freedom from' and 'freedom for' is not something new that humanity is facing. It is being faced by every person who struggles for freedom and suddenly finds freedom. Now that I am free, what am I going to do? Up to now, we were so occupied, so engaged, so very busy that even in our dreams, we were was thinking only of freedom. We never thought about what we will do once we get our freedom.

Getting freedom is not enough. It is the first step — an important step. But something more is needed. We have to become a creator. We have to find some creativity that fulfills our freedom. Otherwise, freedom is empty. We need to either create something or discover something. We can either bring our potential to its full actuality or go inwards to find the source of creation itself.

Freedom is only an opportunity for us. It is not a goal by itself. Freedom gives us the complete opportunity to do whatever we want to do. Now, when we are free, we must use this opportunity — meditation will do, music will do, a sculpture will do, dancing will do, and love will do.

What are we seeking

If we earnestly ask what are we seeking in this restless world, the answer we would get is that we are seeking some sort of peace and some happiness and this we hope to achieve by being successful in life. Most of us would define Sucess as having enough money and a good relationship with our family and friends. So basically we have a pattern of how to live in this world and any external factors that do not allow us to live in that pattern cause fear and anxiety in us, When we demand a particular way of living that itself is a source of fear or a disturbance.. What we call a disturbance is nothing but something we want to get ride of,. we can give it any name but the basic desire for all of us is not to be disturbed, we don't oppose pleasure because there is no disturbance.But we don't see the importance of being disturbed f being inwardly insecure and not being dependet.Because only in insecurity we discover what we are actually and many of us secretly does not want to be discovered what they are. This is because we have been conditioned by the church and the prists to be an ideal person with all the virtues and we have a image of ourselves and anything that makes us move away from that self-image causes us pain. So we always escape from this pain by identifying ourselves with the nation, God, or race or with an idea.

So self-knowledge is understanding onself as one is actually which is the reality and not as one desires to be which is nothing but self-deception. So self-knowledge is a process where we understand what is the truth about us not what we think we are and only in understanding the truth there is a possibility of freedom.What we mean by understanding is that what which is a fact and this is possible by all who wants to have a tranquility of mind as only the truth will free the content of the memory which is nothing but our belief and ideas . As soon as we understand more about ourselves we will realize that all the humans have the same mind, there is nothing different about a person living in one country and another person living in another country,all have the same fear, same pain and all are seeking gratification and that gratification we clothe with an idea, a respectable sounding words like God,truth but all the mind does is seek gratification calling it as God which is the highest point and the lowest point being drink. Realizing this will lead to compassion and only love is something not out of mind and love is the ultimate path that will lead to freedom.

All Travel is self-deception, all seeking is futile

Truth is all the travel is false, where we are, is the place we should be, and where we want to go is the place we are right in this movement. Realizing this truth is not only difficult but almost it is impossible because all our education and conditioning are about achieving or becoming something.

The mind says "Do" something or "Become" something as becoming is always in the future, never in present hence the cunning mind survives. Whether we want to attain power or God, the mind does not mind, as the mind can survive only when there is a desire. The mind needs space to survive and it cannot survive in present. The mind does not mind if we do something, it does not even mind even if we try to get freedom from the mind, as the mind knows that by doing something it can survive. So when a seeker wants to attain freedom, enlightenment, or bliss it is difficult for them to understand this simple truth, so we need to talk about something, a process or knowledge or a technique that will give them hope, but the real truth is all the people who are reading this book would have read many books, so if one is really honest then, they would have come to the simple fact that their search has not ended, Yes it would have given them knowledge even an intellectual understanding of themselves but has this knowledge got transformed into something permanent or everlasting state of bliss or even understanding? An honest answer is "No", The Mind knows this after all the mind is not completely blind, but the search is still on, this is the nature of the mind. Space and time are the creation of the mind and this sustains the illusion of going somewhere.The Mind after seeing that money and power have not given them happiness, needs a new target, the "GOD". So the Mind is not attracted when someone talks about money and it becomes interested only when someone speaks of bliss and enlightenment or when one talks about attaining god.All the religious books speak of attaining something worthwhile something that cannot be taken away something that is everlasting, something that weapon cannot hurt, or something that cannot be taken away. We Search for something great and we think that "GOD" is great as the mind is challenged when the goal is challenging and difficult to attain, what is fun in becoming rich after all becoming buddha is difficult. After all, death will take away everything our money, fame, and power, so if one really sees the working of the mind then we will see that even the spiritual journey is a false one, but this cannot be told to a person who has not even tried anything and failed, that is the challenge in the path, we have to try even if we are not successful as it will take us to a state of mind that knows that it is futile but that state can be attained only by trying and failing there is no shortcut.Then there is a realization from the frustration of the failure of the trying that the mind cannot grasp anything intelligent so it definitely cannot grasp God and this realization only can make the mind silent, not our discipline or will or effort.There is no need for any effort or process or method, after all, what we are seeking is not far from us, it is near to us, in fact, we are part of it, It is something far that needs to be attained what is within does not need any process, it is only the question of understanding, it is the nature of the mind to notice only things what are outside as all our understanding comes through our senses and senses by nature are outbound as they have been created for survival purpose. So if we want to travel inside, there is no need for senses, one just has to close their eyes and sit doing nothing, then something inside us will explode.